YOU'RE SO INVITED

YOU'RE SO INVITED

PANIC LESS, PLAY MORE, AND GET YOUR PARTY ON

r.s.v.p. Cheryl Najafi

CherylStyle

Published by

St. Martin's Press

Produced by

MELCHER
MEDIA

Photography by

Lisa Romerein

For my colleagues, friends, and family,
who inspire me to follow my dreams.
—Cheryl

For information, address St. Martin's Press, 175 Fifth Avenue, New York, N.Y. 10010.

www.stmartins.com

Design: Wink, Inc.

Photographer: Lisa Romerein

Secondary photo credits, which constitute an extension of the copyright page, appear on page 192.

Library of Congress Cataloging-in-Publication Data is available upon request.

ISBN 978-1-250-01199-2

First Edition: April 2012

10 9 8 7 6 5 4 3 2

CONTENTS

General Preparation Tips & Advice

I know the concept of throwing a party and wanting everything to be just so. You want to wow your guests, and have them leave thinking you're the superhero host of the Western world. And that's all good and great, but it's a ton of pressure. Bringing people into your home is such a personal thing. I know it's easier said than done, but try not to take it too seriously and just have fun with it. After all, they're your good friends and want you to succeed, right? To get you in the mood to party, here are seven rules for throwing a party without wanting to throw yourself off a ledge:

1. TAKE BABY STEPS

If you're new to entertaining, don't jump in with your spouse's 40th birthday party. Start small. Invite a few of your best friends over for a Chinese takeout party. Surround yourself with people who love you and are rooting for you.

2. DRUM UP A THEME

When you title an event, you instantly elevate it, and the party takes on a personality of its own. Say you decide to throw a Funny Hat party. The very idea makes people feel comfortable because they're all on the same page. Once I threw an over-the-hill, hiking-themed 30th birthday party for myself, and people still talk about it. We had a chili cook-off and a tent you had to climb in to get dessert. We ate off blue tin camping plates and drank out of canteens. Oh, and khakis were required attire. It's such a fun process to think of a theme and see how far you can carry it.

3. BREAK THE RULES

Who says you must serve wine from wineglasses? When it comes to parties, I'm always a little irreverent. If you're supposed to do something, I'm going to make sure I do it differently. A few years ago my husband had important clients coming over. I set a formal table because I was "supposed to," but then I served kid food for dinner. We had mini gourmet pizzas, mac and cheese in adorable little antique French pots, chicken-finger skewers, and for dessert, hot fudge sundaes with maraschino cherries. Everyone loved it and kept wondering what the next course would be.

4. EXPECT THAT SOMETHING WILL GO WRONG—AND BE OK WITH IT

I love this quote from Carl Jung: "In all chaos there is a cosmos, in all disorder a secret order." It's so true—things aren't always as they seem. When you host a party, the only thing you can count on is that something will inevitably go wrong. But how you handle the situation will dictate how successful the party is. Whatever happens, just go with it, because more often than not, the thing you thought was such a disaster could turn out to be the party's

defining moment (in a good way). A happy accident, if you will. When I'm entertaining, I use the metaphor that I'm driving a bumper car. If I hit something, I change direction and go in another, but I'm still moving. Just shift—if it doesn't work, do something else. One time all the lighting in my house was wackadoo—all the bulbs were at 100 percent brightness. It seriously looked like a landing strip. I made light of it (sorry), and everyone got a good laugh. It's so much better to do that than to apologize for it.

5. FOLLOW YOUR BLISS

So much about being a happy host depends on trusting your instincts. If you feel strongly about something, don't get swayed by what others think is best. Truly listen to how they frame things—sometimes there's a caveat, a warning, a roadblock. Don't get me wrong: I'll listen to advice, but a "warning" to me is a challenge. Some people hear a warning and they back up. I hear a warning and put my armor on. Instead, focus on the positive and it'll propel you to move forward. Think of it this way: Which drip are you going to put the bucket under? The one with the nice, positive things people are saying, or the one with all the caveats, warnings, and concerns that people are giving you? I choose to put it under the first bucket.

6. FOCUS ON YOUR STRENGTHS

Don't think you have to be an expert in all things party. I say, pick one thing you're great at and do it well. Pay attention to what makes your heart beat faster (What makes you feel confident? What do people say you're great at?). Hone those skills to become even better. To get a sense of your strengths and style, it helps to make a list of things you hate and things you love.

7. FOCUS ON YOUR GUESTS

All of my ideas for stress-free entertaining are guided by my philosophy that you should enjoy your guests. When I take the focus off of trying to be the perfect host and funnel that energy into making my guests feel special, the pressure to be perfect dissolves.

THE FINAL COUNTDOWN

Whether you're throwing a casual get-together or a sit-down for 20,
consult this checklist of what to do when.

Three weeks before

- Come up with a theme.

- Nail down your guest list.

- Send out invites.

- Think about the food: finger-food only or sit-down style?

Two weeks before

- Go around your house and take inventory of table-cloths, napkins, glasses, and plates.

- Order anything you might need from a party supply store, like chairs or tables, heat lamps, or even a coat rack to save your bed from a barrage of jackets.

One week before

- Launder tablecloths and napkins, if necessary, and clean all dishware and silverware.

- Order (or pick up) wine and alcohol from the liquor store. You'll need about three bottles of wine for every four guests—it's best to buy more than less; you never know if Uncle Al will try to drink you under the table. For alcohol, figure guests will have about two drinks an hour.

Forty-eight hours before

- Think about a lighting plan. Replace bright bulbs with lower-wattage versions. Screw in a few pink bulbs, which give off a rosy glow and make all skin tones look good.

Twenty-four hours before

- Clean the house. Pay special attention to the spots guests will notice: the bathroom, living room, dining room, and anything at eye level.

- Store valuables and fragile items in a locked cabinet (or at least in the back of an out-of-the way closet).

- Set the table and bar. It's nice to wake up the day of the party and know this step is done.

Two hours before

- Take a shower. You can always prepare in front of your guests but you can't shower in front of them.

- Scan your medicine cabinet to preempt any snoopers. Put medication you don't want people to see in a bedroom dresser drawer.

One hour before

- Uncork bottles of wine to let them breathe (and ensure you're not fumbling with the bottle opener while trying to kiss Aunt Lucy on the cheek).

Thirty minutes before

- Turn on the music. Put the finishing touches (aka garnishes) on your dishes.

- Roll up delicate rugs and store in a closet.

- Set out lots of coasters, especially on unfinished wood tables.

- Put cocktail napkins on every side of your coffee table so guests don't feel the need to wipe their paws on your couch. If you have stain-prone upholstered pieces—like a silk sofa, say—toss a slipcover or a throw on top.

- Place welcome mats outside—and inside—the front door to catch dirt before it makes its way onto your cream flokati.

Fifteen minutes before

- Take ice out of the freezer and pour into ice buckets.

- Turn off overhead lights, dim others, and light candles. Be sure to position candles away from windows (drafts could cause a flare-up) and anything flammable like curtains or lampshades. Stash a small fire extinguisher in a kitchen cupboard—just in case!

Right before

- Put on your heels, check your lipstick—and make sure nothing's in your teeth!

Some people are itchin' to be in the kitchen. Others are blissed out with take-out. Some people can decorate all day. Others just want to call it a day. When it comes to entertaining, chances are you fall into one of these host profiles:

You have a panic attack every time the doorbell rings. You've never hosted a party before and are paralyzed by the thought of planning one. In fact, you don't even know where to begin. Not to fret! The parties in this book will show you what to do every step of the way—from choosing a theme for your celebration to creating special invitations to orchestrating engaging party activities. Want to know where to start? How about our mix-and-mingle with a jingle Holiday Coffee Drop-In? It's a no-fail, no-stress party that helps you easily slip into the hostess role.

You've got a few parties under your belt, but occasionally you struggle with the specifics, like how to pace your party, repurpose items hidden away in your closet and attic, determine how many bottles of wine to buy for a certain number of guests, and deal with last-minute cancellations. Guess what? You're in luck! This book is chock-full of party planning tips, tools, and tricks, plus a variety of ideas to expand your repertoire. Consider stretching your entertaining muscle by throwing our Guys-Only Scotch & Cigars Gathering. It has everything a man could want—except a woman!

You'll stop at nothing to shock and awe your guests, so it stands to reason that you're an outrageous, outgoing, out-of-the-box thinker. This book will make your livin'-large reputation legendary, with parties that are slightly irreverent and that feature unexpected playful twists—whether it's the party theme, the creative invitations, or the crazy-fun activity suggestions. Why not stir up a good time by hosting our Martini Birthday Bash? In addition to the chilled martinis, every course of the meal is served in martini glasses, making the event feel lighthearted and irreverent. Bottoms up!

You're a take-charge person who's always in control—whether you're coordinating, creating, or crafting. You like to plan and execute every last detail of a party with precision. Churn the butter? Check. Embroider the tablecloths? Check. Make the party decor? Check. Direct guest activities? Check. You'll love how the parties in this book cover every detail of planning a successful celebration—from invitations to libations. Since you're the type who doesn't lose her gourd easily, why not take on our Elegant Thanksgiving Potluck? You'll give thanks for being so detail-oriented.

You leave everything until the last minute, have no problem entertaining in your sweats, and believe paper plates and takeout are two modern conveniences you simply can't live without. You barely lift a finger once guests arrive—not because you don't care, but because you'd rather spend time talking to them than fussing with hostess duties. Strip away a hectic day and host our Yen-for-Zen Garden Get-Together. This down-to-earth party is all about creating a warm, inviting atmosphere that mixes backyard finds, garden-fresh fare, and mix-and-match dishes. Take a deep breath and go for it!

Still not sure what your personal host profile is? Go to CherylStyle.com and take our quick quiz to find out, then learn how to throw a bash that won't clash with your style.

Decorating & Decor

VASES ARE BORING:

11 Unexpected Vessels for Flowers to Fill

I rarely use a vase. I'd rather look around the house for things I can repurpose. Take, for example...

1. High-top sneaker: Great for a boy's birthday party.

2. Cigar box: Fill with small flowers and they'll look like they're growing out of the box.

3. Vintage metal coffeepots.

4. Pretty patterned teapots.

5. Jam jars, honey jars, or Mason jars: great for wildflowers and sunflowers.

6. Galvanized buckets.

7. Pretty wine bottles: Calla lilies look gorgeous in these, because the thin neck of the bottle keeps them upright.

8. Beer bottles: Seriously! Stick a bunch of wildflowers in a bottle of Bass Ale and you'll know what I mean.

9. Vegetables: Think carved-out pumpkins, cabbages, and peppers.

10. Fishbowls.

11. Red wagon: Place outside your house and fill it with geraniums. Now, *that's* a welcome wagon!

MOOD LIGHTING: 5 WAYS TO CREATE A SUBTLE LIGHTING SCHEME

1. Switch off the overheads—they're way too glaring for a party. Focus on table and floor lamps instead. In the kitchen, for example, put a table lamp on the kitchen counter and flick on the vent hood or under-cabinet lighting.

2. Replace those 100-watts with chiller 60-watts.

3. Consider your theme. If you're rocking a '60s or '70s vibe, go the lava lamp route. If you're having an alfresco luau, bring on the tiki torches.

4. You can never have enough candles. Line the mantel, put one in the bathroom, and fill those silver candlesticks with votives (and actually light them).

5. Play around with mirrors to bounce light around the room.

YOUR PARTY TOOLKIT: 7 SAVING GRACES

It's good to have a few go-to items that you can always turn to in a pinch, whether you need to spruce up a centerpiece or make flowers look more presentable. Here are the seven tools I seriously couldn't live without:

1. **Raffia.** I tie almost everything with raffia—from fresh flowers to napkins.
2. **Burlap.** I keep bolts of colored burlap in my closet, and use it for table runners, place mats, even wrapping the base of a planter to give it more texture. I don't sew, so this is perfect for me.
3. **Boas.** I'll cut boas into 2-inch pieces and pepper a table with them. Or I'll stuff wheatgrass inside an antique pot, fill it with bright Gerber daisies, and then have a piece of a boa sticking out.
4. **Glue dots.** They're excellent for securing a candle in a holder.
5. **Floral wire.** This thin bendy wire helps you manipulate things, like keep a napkin treatment in place.
6. **Floral foam.** It's great for helping you make a vase out of things that aren't typically meant to hold water; just put a bit of water at the bottom of the vessel and the foam will drink it up.
7. **Silicone jelly.** You can add these dried granules to water and they'll expand like Jell-O to help preserve flowers.

One of the easiest ways to make a table feel special and original? Use what I call thematic tension. It's about blending colors and textures to create a unique look that still feels unified. Here are a few tips to get you started:

• **Mix rough with polished, matte with shiny.** One party I like to throw is called Potted—it's a farmer's market feel with a buffet table packed with large terra-cotta pots as the serving vessels, gardening tools as the serving utensils, and bread in rustic metal baskets, with stacked saucers as the dinner plates. When you bring your terra-cotta "plate" to the table to sit down, you place it on a beautiful china charger. Next to that is a gorgeous sparkly crystal wineglass, so you get that great contrast of rugged with refined. But limit yourself to two main textures—throwing in that third texture can make the table feel like a hodgepodge.

Some other textures to play around with:

glossy lacquer trays topped with pewter bowls

a textured linen tablecloth with sleek glass plates

modern vinyl place mats on a rustic bare wood dining table

colorful fringed napkins on a crisp white cotton tablecloth

burlap napkins tied with elegant strands of pearls

fancy china paired with casual water-glasses for wine

• **Keep color intensities consistent.** You don't want pink pastel chair cushions with bright blue centerpieces. Instead, if you have a chartreuse tablecloth, pair it with bright eggplant-colored napkins that are of a similar color value. That way, the eye isn't jarred.

• **Create relationships.** To make sure your table doesn't look like a mishmash, something should always relate to something else so that there's a connection. A red charger can speak to red centerpiece flowers, for example.

• **Toss in a surprise.** Don't always do the obvious thing—be a bit of a rebel. If you're throwing a wings-and-beer party, instead of setting the table with big and burly beer mugs, use tall delicate pilsner glasses instead. It'll make the table feel lighter—and less expected.

• **Tone it down a bit.** When there's a lot going on, it's always good to keep one thing simple to let the eye rest. For instance, if you're doing a big ol' mash-up with different patterns of salad plates, dinner plates, and chargers, make sure the centerpiece flowers are all the same variety and color (pink peonies rather than a spring bouquet, say) to give the table a breather.

Food & Drink

Never know how much stuff to buy? Check out this handy chart (for a four-hour party).

Guests	10	20	30
Wine	8 bottles	16 bottles	24 bottles
Alcohol	4 bottles	8 bottles	12 bottles
Hors d'oeuvres (dinner party)	60 pieces	120 pieces	180 pieces
Hors d'oeuvres (cocktail party)	120 pieces	240 pieces	360 pieces
Ice	10 pounds	20 pounds	30 pounds

READY FOR ANYTHING: STOCKING UP THE PANTRY, FRIDGE, AND FREEZER

You'll feel better as a host knowing you're prepared for whatever comes your way (unexpected guests? impromptu dinner party?). For the fridge and freezer, carve out a corner just for party supplies, and tell your family it's off limits! For the pantry, designate a couple of shelves in your main storage area or use a pretty armoire. Consider keeping cocktail napkins, place mats, serveware, and wine openers in here, too.

In the pantry:
• Boxes of crackers.
• Breadsticks (preferably with sea salt!).
• Jars of artichokes, olive tapenade, stuffed grape leaves, beets, and roasted sweet peppers.
• Wasabi peas.
• Pomegranate seeds: They're great for adding color to a dish.
• Almonds, pine nuts, pistachio nuts, and walnuts.
• Various dips, pesto, and onion paste.
• Dried fruits: These are decadent paired with cheese.
• Canned chicken: Use it to whip up a chicken salad with grapes, dates, or almonds, then serve on crackers. I like to use plain yogurt with olive oil rather than mayo. It's not like having fresh chicken—but it's better than tuna.

In the freezer:
• Vanilla ice cream: Can a dessert be more simple or perfect? Serve up some scoops in wineglasses or teacups and top with pirouette cookies.
• Biscotti: These cookies just seem to get better in the freezer. I serve them directly from the freezer—they're so crunchy. If someone shows up for dessert, just pull them out. They're tough to keep around in my house, but I still try.

In the fridge:

• Cheese: Unopened cheese can last for months.

• Jars of veggies, like baby corn and asparagus: It's better to keep these in the fridge than the pantry—they don't taste as good at room temperature. You can pull them out and know they'll be crisp and refreshing.

• Pepperoni: Pair with cheese and olives and you're all set.

• Olives: I love going to the olive bar and picking out exotic olives to keep on hand. They're fun and flavorful—you can get ones that are infused with pepper or stuffed with garlic.

• Fig jam: It's a perfect complement to cheese. Your family isn't likely to eat it otherwise, so you won't go reaching for it and find it's not there—trust me!

• Marinara sauce: It should be good enough to drink. You can do so much with it, from jazzing up a baked potato to creating mini pizzas or bruschetta. I get mine from Trader Joe's.

• Capers: I like keeping these on hand for bagels.

• Uncooked tortillas: Poke holes in them with a fork, and put olive oil around the edges to make them crusty. Top with marinara sauce, fresh mozzarella, and dried oregano flakes and bake at 350°F for 10 minutes. They're the most amazing low-carb pizzas you've ever had. A real kid-pleaser too.

• Tollhouse cookie dough: When making cookies (or Gruyère cheese puffs, for that matter), I always like to underbake a batch and freeze them. Before heating them up in the oven, sprinkle with coarse sea salt and you'll elevate them to gourmet status.

TAKEOUT FAKEOUT:
10 NO-FAIL CROWD-PLEASING DISHES YOU CAN ORDER IN (AND SPRUCE UP)

1. **Steak bites:** Skewer with toothpicks and dip into pesto.
2. **Thin-crust pizza:** Use it as a cracker and top with goodies you'd put in an antipasto, like pepperoncini, salami, and olives.
3. **Yellowtail sashimi:** Garnish with slices of jalapeño pepper and dollops of cactus jelly. Remember to keep this dish cold—place a bowl of ice underneath.
4. **Macaroni and cheese:** Sprinkle with toasted bread crumbs and serve in clear glass votives.
5. **Chinese pot stickers:** Serve with a selection of mustards (yellow, Dijon, extra spicy).
6. **Chili:** Pour it over baked potatoes, and serve with toppings like bacon, shredded cheese, and broccoli florets.
7. **Bite-sized crab cakes:** Serve on sliced cucumbers and top with lemon butter (whip together a stick of softened butter with a teaspoon of lemon peel and a tablespoon of lemon juice).
8. **Cooked shrimp:** Skewer the little guys with cherry tomatoes, cucumbers, and black olives.
9. **French fries:** Spritz with vinegar and sprinkle with sea salt.
10. **Lasagna:** Keep a stock of medium-size ramekins in your cupboard and drop them off at a caterer or a favorite market. Ask to have them filled with individual portions of lasagna.
    You could also do this with potpie, macaroni and cheese, or eggplant parmigiana.
    Developing relationships with local vendors is the key to dinner on the fly.

5 FOOLPROOF PARTY PLATTERS

1. The Cheese, Please: Camembert, Manchego, triple crème Brie, and Stilton with honey, pistachios, and baguette slices.

2. The Italian Connection: Genoa salami, smoked mozzarella, basil leaves, roasted red peppers, and large Italian olives.

3. The Meat Lovers: Salami, ham, roast beef, spicy mustard, cornichons, and artichoke hearts.

4. The Big Dipper: Crab dip with fresh veggies, tzatziki with pita chips, seven-layer dip with tortilla chips.

5. The Fruit Loot: Sliced strawberries, bananas, kiwi, peaches, and pears with vanilla yogurt.

Going-Away Roast

*For a pal who is skipping town or a
favorite coworker who landed a new gig...*

It's bittersweet when a friend heads to another state or a colleague switches jobs. But there's no need to be all down about it. Instead, use this opportunity to throw a lighthearted roast that celebrates the fun times you've had and the new ones yet to come. At this party, bubble wrap is your new best friend, while a muted cardboard-box palette lets you work in bright hits of color, like red flowers cascading out of a festive centerpiece of packing material, paper plates, and plastic forks. All as if he were packed up and ready to move, and we had all dropped by to say good-bye. Parting doesn't have to be such sweet sorrow after all!

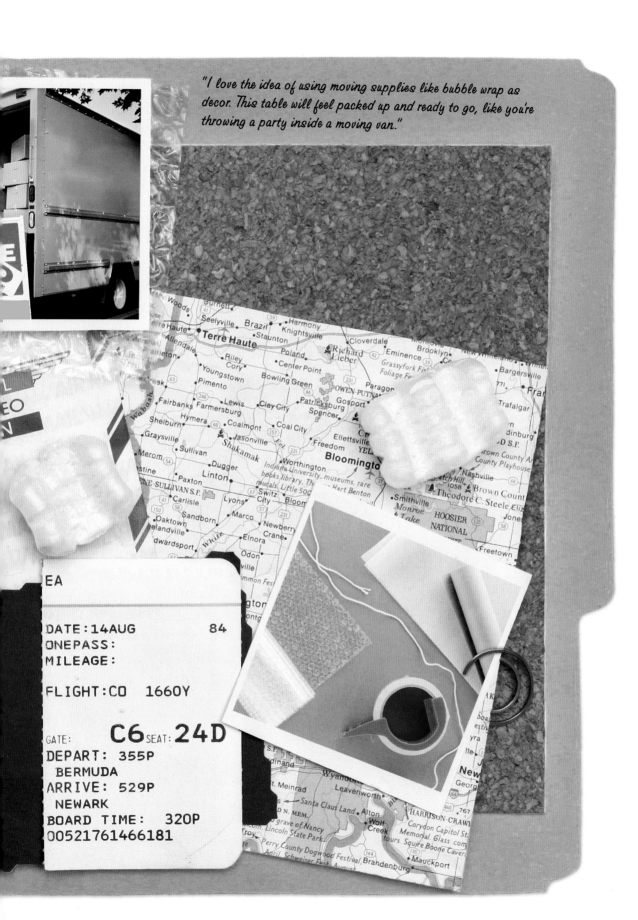

"I love the idea of using moving supplies like bubble wrap as decor. This table will feel packed up and ready to go, like you're throwing a party inside a moving van."

EA

DATE:14AUG   84
ONEPASS:
MILEAGE:

FLIGHT:CO 1660Y

GATE: C6 SEAT: 24D
DEPART: 355P
  BERMUDA
ARRIVE: 529P
  NEWARK
BOARD TIME: 320P
00521761466181

"When my good friend and neighbor Jeff told me he was moving across the country, I wanted to honor him with something special. Jeff is obsessed with fishing and always talks about his adventures on the lake, so I created a fish-friendly corkboard—complete with a singing fish—of well wishes that guests e-mailed me, and hung them from lures that I bought at a tackle store. I tweaked the wording so that everything related to fishing. If someone said, 'I can't believe my best friend is moving. I'm going to miss you so much!' I'd translate that as 'I'm going to miss you 'this' much. You are my bass friend!' When he arrived, I put a fisherman's hat on his head and showed him the board. It was a great way to kick off the party."

FRAGILE—HANDLE WITH CARE

Think packaging supply store meets picnic: beige napkins secured with FRAGILE stickers, and recyclable plastic plates, bowls, and utensils. Cork place mats add subtle texture (the ones I used are from Ikea, but you could also buy cork at a crafts store and cut pieces out yourself). Each setting features a large envelope with postage markings; you can send some to yourself to get the official "stamps." (If someone's moving to another country, decorate with foreign stamps.) Print or write each guest's name on THIS END UP stickers, available at CherylStyle.com/book.

GET PERSONAL

If a friend is moving to Spain or has a penchant for Spanish food, say, include a cava toast and serve tapas. Place a nice notebook on a table for guests to write phone numbers, addresses, and farewell words. Consider printing out the person's new address on small pieces of paper for everyone to put in their wallets. You can also have guests write notes on postcards and later send them to the honoree's address for a pleasant surprise once he gets to the new location.

THE SECRETS OF THROWING A RIOTOUS ROAST

Roasts, if done well, can be so poignant. What makes it a hit or a flop? Think of it this way: poor roasts make fun of people's weaknesses, while great roasts compliment the person's good qualities in a funny way. The idea is that you're showing the honoree how much you love him by making light of his "flaws," but there's a difference between affectionately mocking and brutally shocking. The best result is when you almost touch the line but don't cross it—make him squirm, but just a little bit. Here, ten strategies for throwing a roast your guest of honor will remember— rather than try to forget.

1. Keep the surprises for another party.
Bring up the idea of a roast to gauge the guest of honor's reaction. Tell your roastee that he'll get a chance to counter-roast—this is payback time when he gets his turn to have the last word.

2. Compile a varied guest list.
When you have everyone from colleagues and cousins to old friends and new neighbors participating in the roast, you'll get a broad view of the honoree and an insight into his various walks of life.

3. Emphasize short but sweet.
Instruct your roasters to keep their speech under two minutes. Jokes that go over best are ones that have a setup and punch line in a sentence or two.

4. Play it safe (perhaps).
If you're concerned that the guest of honor may take offense at certain comments, ask everyone to e-mail you a copy of their toast. If something seems suspect, ask the person to tone it down. If you want to keep it strictly PG-13, ask guests not to say anything they wouldn't say in front of their children, mother, or boss.

5. Make it personal.
Once I threw a party for my friend Stephanie, who always wears black and white. I asked everyone to come dressed as she dresses. Everyone showed up in black and white. Her mom even came dressed in Stephanie's white prom dress. They just nailed her.

6. Serve dinner before the roast—and dole out the drinks.
In case the roast goes longer than planned, you'll want to make sure guests are well fed and a tad tipsy to encourage raucous laughter.

7. Bring those who can't attend in on the action.
Have them send in funny stories that you can relay. Tell them to think about quirky anecdotes and funny stories that will make everyone think, *That is SO him*. The best jokes are the ones that everyone in the room gets, so keep it general enough for the mix of people in the crowd.

8. Be the master of the roast, keeper of the zoo.
To kick off the festivities, get up there and poke fun at yourself to make the roastee feel like he's not the only one feeling the heat. Start with a harmless joke: "It's actually really nice to talk to you today, Jeff, considering I've been talking behind your back for years."

9. Bring on the props.
Use a gavel or noisemaker to put an end to out-of-line or snooze-worthy speeches, or toss a beach ball at him when you're telling the story of when he lost his trunks in the ocean.

10. But seriously . . . end on a high (touching) note.
As roastmaster, wrap it up by saying something you truly love about the guest of honor and emphasize how much he'll be missed.

A floral centerpiece sprouting plastic utensils sets the tongue-in-cheek mood. When it comes to tableware for an outdoor party, unbreakable = unbeatable.

SIGNATURE DRINK: THE BYE, BYE BIRDIE
(AKA THE PERFECT TOM COLLINS)

To prepare it, you'll need:

1½ tablespoons fresh lemon juice

1 teaspoon sugar—the finer the better
  so that it melts easily

1½ ounces gin (equal to one jigger)

Club soda

Slices of lemon and lime

Directions:

Fill a Tom Collins glass (or any tall
thin glass) with lemon juice and
sugar; stir vigorously. Add gin. Toss
in enough ice cubes to fill the glass.
Stir, then top off with club soda
and garnish with lemon and lime.

Fix It and Forget It: 5 Cocktails to Serve from a Drink Dispenser

(These are measurements for one drink, so just multiply by the number of guests, and figure that each guest will have at least 1½ drinks.)

1. Mai Tai: 1 ounce dark rum, 1 ounce Amaretto liqueur, 3 ounces orange juice, 3 ounces pineapple juice, 1 dash grenadine syrup. **2. Cable Car:** 1½ ounces Captain Morgan Original Spiced Rum, ¾ ounce Orange Curaçao, 1½ ounces sour mix. **3. Gimlet:** 2 ounces gin, ⅔ ounce Rose's Lime Juice. **4. Americano:** 1½ ounces Campari, 1½ ounces sweet vermouth, club soda. **5. Sex on the Beach**: 2 ounces vodka, 1 ounce peach schnapps, a splash of grapefruit juice, a splash of cranberry juice.

This is a gorgeous salad that's so flavorful and extremely easy to make. When you roast beets, the skins act as a sealant, holding in the juiciness as well as the bright color. I rub olive oil and sea salt on mine before cooking.

Directions:

1. To make this pop-of-color salad, you'll need two baby beets per person. (If you can only find large beets, figure one per person, and quarter them after roasting so that they're easier to eat.) **2.** Wash the beets well and cut the stalk so that it's about a half-inch long. (The stalk is edible and delicious, and it gives the salad a more rustic look.) **3.** Keeping the skins on, wrap each beet individually in tinfoil—this allows for faster cooking and sweats the skin so that you can easily peel it off. **4.** Place beets on a baking sheet and put in a 350°F oven for about an hour to an hour and a half, or until the beets are tender when poked with a fork. Let cool for 15 minutes. **5.** Rub beets with your fingers to peel the skins off. Slice each in half lengthwise (straight down from the stalk). You can marinate the beets if you want, but they're really sweet when roasted like this, so they don't need much doctoring. **6.** To make the salad, mix together baby spinach and sprigs of wild thyme. Toss the beets onto the greens, and add a simple dressing of lemon, olive oil, salt, and pepper.

PULL-OFFABLE PUDDING

Don't be afraid to serve basics—those tried-and-true dishes that make guests feel comfortable. People really go crazy for the simple things, like chocolate pudding they haven't had for 15 years—it reminds them of being a kid. With a garnish and a pop of color, a simple dish can morph into something fun and unexpected.

Directions:

1. Buy a large tub of chocolate pudding or make it yourself from a box. Carefully spoon pudding into each wineglass or, for less mess, use a piping bag. (If you don't have one, create your own by cutting one corner of a plastic baggie.) **2.** Fill each cup two-thirds with pudding, then top with a dollop of whipped cream and half a strawberry. For other garnishes, try blueberries, raspberries, slices of banana, chocolate shavings (use a cheese grater), sprinkles, candy, almonds, cookie crumbs, or vanilla wafers. **3.** Wrap the bottom of each glass with perforated packing paper, tucked inside itself to secure. Stick FRAGILE and THIS SIDE UP stickers on a box fitted with a glass-divider insert. Place glasses inside. The guests then unpack their dessert!

Set a festive mood for your guest of honor
with this homemade throne.

CRAFTING A CARDBOARD THRONE

Start with a large shipping box and use packing tape to make the side flaps stand up. Place a bubble-wrapped chair inside the box and fill gaps on all sides with packing material; secure it all with FRAGILE tape. Use a generous piece of inflatable packaging as the seat cushion and tape a small box to one side as a cup holder. Voilà!

Party Highlights

TRICKS FOR OUTDOOR ENTERTAINING

Keep food cold by putting bowls of ice underneath—use a dish that's slightly larger than the one you're serving from but the same shape.

Camouflage a garbage can behind a plant or put a garbage bag in a pretty vase, planter, or urn. Play to your theme; if you're having a luau, wrap a grass skirt around the pail.

Cover food with mesh domes to keep flies away; you can repurpose colanders or strainers.

Scatter citronella candles around the yard to ward off insects. Incense sticks have worked well for me, too.

Place votive candles in paper bags (filled with a bit of sand) to block the wind.

PACKING PEANUTS RAFFLE

Fill a big cardboard box or oversized vase with foam peanuts and have guests guess how many are in there.

WANT TO GET THE PARTY POPPIN'?

Give each guest a big sheet of bubble wrap and tell them to put it on the floor in front of them. At the count of three, everyone has to jump on it and start popping—the first to pop all their bubbles wins.

Happy Accidents

STICKY SITUATION: One of the people giving a toast starts to get nervous, bobbles his words, and freezes.

HOSTESS RECOVERY: Grab the bubble wrap, start popping, and say, "This is a bubble-wrap pause. Does anyone else need to pop some bubble wrap?" And, of course, a few guests will. With the attention off, the speaker regains composure and finishes up with a laugh. Now the party will really get popping (sorry).

STICKY SITUATION: The roastee is visibly offended by something someone has said.

HOSTESS RECOVERY: Use your noise-maker to cut off the toast, and get on up there. Start pulling out your most heart-felt, honest feelings about this person. Soon, the guest of honor will be touched, and so will the audience. A truly memorable affair, indeed.

TWISTS ON A THEME: MORE PARTY IDEAS FROM CHERYLSTYLE.COM

BREAK THE TAPE ESCAPE: In this case, the retiree is breaking through crime scene tape as the host plays detective to find out "who done it." The guests arrive and check in by being fingerprinted. The buffet table is loaded with evidence and evidence-gathering tools. The signature drink is the Dick Tracy (you'll be talking to your watch!), and tables feature photos of the retiree who has been "framed"!

HE'S LEAF-ING!: Sometimes going-away parties are about moving on to a new stage in life, like this one for a recent graduate. This outdoor celebration features the planting of a young tree in the grad's honor, and giving seedlings to the guests so they can watch their tree grow along with the graduate.

HE'S A KEY'PER: Take inspiration from this revved-up guy's birthday party set in a garage and adapt it to a going-away party where you wish you could key'p the guy around—around the garage, that is! This celebration's ignition switch is a mechanic-themed buffet and place setting, plus fun-filled remote-control car races in the driveway.

Yen-for-Zen Garden Get-Together

*For a casual, back-to-basics
celebration with friends...*

In our hectic day-to-day lives, there's something to be said for stripping away all of the noise, surrounding yourself with those you feel most comfortable with, and really getting back to basics. That's exactly what this party is all about: creating a warm, inviting atmosphere with breathe-easy decor that mixes backyard finds; simple, rustic pieces; and classic china-cupboard staples. A table adorned with textured objects that beg to be touched makes people feel instantly comfortable—like they're not going to mess something up or have to behave themselves. And decorating with personal pieces gives guests a snapshot of your world. We're all a combination of various elements—why not put your favorite pieces together to give your guests a sense of what really makes you tick? Prepare to be enlightened.

"Using elements from the garden, whether it's smooth black rocks or sprigs of mint, turns this 'shut out the noise' Zen-like party into a textural treat."

" I designed this party for Mariel Hemingway to celebrate the launch of the new company she founded with her partner, Bobby Williams. The company, WillingWay— a combination of the couple's last names—is a line of products to help inspire people to lead happy, healthy lives. Mariel wanted to share her venture with friends and family in a relaxed setting that included items from her cherished garden and combined her grandfather's antiques with the Zen-inspired dishware that reflects who she is today."

CREATE AN ECLECTIC AESTHETIC

Experiment with mixing and matching different objects around your home. First swing open the cupboards and dust off that china. Most of us pick our china and wonder years later, *Why the heck did I choose that? It doesn't reflect who I am today*. But it's china—you're not going to get more just because it doesn't reflect your current style—you get it once and that's that. Try complementing it with newer items that represent how you've evolved. Mariel inherited floral Limoges from her grandmother and silverware from her beloved grandfather. They were resonant with stories—but even though they don't necessarily represent her style today, they do reflect her family's past.

The items that truly speak to her now are more clean-lined and simple, so we used these Zen-inspired pieces to bring her own sense of style to the table. The result is a unique combination of colors and textures, and a seamless transition between old and new. To make the varied mix feel cohesive, use a crisp background: here, we used a bright orange table runner to tie all the other colors together and give the raw wood table a shot of adrenaline. Another tip: When setting the table, take into consideration the food you're serving. When poured into the turquoise bowls, split pea soup offers a gorgeous blue-on-green color explosion. Below are a few more mix-and-match tableware tricks:

PAIR SOLIDS WITH PATTERNS

The key is to keep one main color consistent, then train your eye to look for similarities between seemingly disparate items. On this table, the flowery, feminine china and spare turquoise bowls don't immediately feel like they match, but look closely and you'll see they're both trimmed in gold, and that the blue bowl picks up the color of one of the flowers in the china.

GO FOR A VARIETY OF SHAPES

Square and oval trivets break up the roundness of dinnerware and teacups and give them a little edge.

VARY TEXTURES

Shiny glass looks exquisite on a rough-hewn wood table; polished silverware really shines on top of nubby napkins.

CONNECT WITH THE EARTH

Head outside armed with a basket—everything you need to decorate your party is free for the taking. You can tuck fragrant herbs into a napkin or use shiny black rocks as name cards, like we did. Mariel and I wrote words that have meaning to her, like *love, courage,*

Right: A green salad is a nice, light accompaniment to a meat dish. Opposite: Sleek Zen bowls pop against a rough-hewn wooden table.

and *harmony,* on the rocks with a silver pen and placed one at each setting. Then we put another set of rocks in a bowl near the entrance for each guest to take. The rock you picked dictated where you'd sit. Mariel believes in trusting the universe, so whatever stone guests pulled, it was their prompting to sit in that spot. You can also use rocks as trivets—look for large, flat ones—or for lining the base of a powder-room sink to give guests a Zen-like experience while washing their hands. Scout around for sculptural branches, which you can set in a metal vase for a gorgeous juxtaposition of earthy and shiny. To add a touch of green to the table, slide leaves underneath clear glass dinner plates or use them as coasters.

TAP INTO YOUR INNER HOST

Tailor the party to your own specific tastes. If you're obsessed with jewelry, say, use bangles as napkin rings and pin brooches to the tablecloth. If you're a photography nut, use pictures of guests as name cards and set out disposable cameras to inspire fun shots. And if you're a tea lover, repurpose vintage teapots as vases and wrap pretty tea bags around napkins instead of napkin rings.

THE ZEN APPROACH TO PARTY HOSTING

When it comes to entertaining, the best way to find Zen is to be prepared. Great ideas are a dime a dozen. The execution is where people get stalled. The key is to think through what you're going to need so that you're not scrambling at the last minute. It's all about having a mental checklist so that when the guests arrive, you've done it all and you can just relax and enjoy. Make lists to help organize your thoughts. Write down how many people will be there, how much food and alcohol you'll need, what kinds of songs you'll want to play, and make sure you make those playlists and that the iPod dock is where it needs to be. Now take a few long, deep breaths before the first *ding-dong* of the doorbell!

SMART FURNITURE ARRANGEMENTS TO KEEP THE PARTY FLOWING

- Position the bar across the room from the food buffet to minimize traffic jams. Pull both tables a few inches from the wall to allow access from both sides.
- For a cocktail party where you'll want guests to mingle, don't feel like you need a chair for every guest—one chair for every three or four guests should do it. Create seating clusters of about four or five seats each.
- If you do need extra seating, pull out folding chairs after most guests have shown up so you don't block an entryway. Have these on hand in a nearby closet.
- Nothing's worse than not knowing what to do with your garbage, so make sure you put little bowls or a glass where food is—and bait it (put a little wrapper in there so people know it's for garbage).

THE GUESTS ARE COMING!
THE GUESTS ARE COMING!
SEVEN WAYS TO CALM DOWN THE DAY
OF THE PARTY

1. Run around the block. A brisk walk is fine too.
2. Get a mani/pedi.
3. Take a nap.
4. Do a yoga pose—headstands are great!
5. Listen to your favorite music. Classical is always soothing, but if hip-hop gets your party on, go for it!
6. Invite a friend over to help with last-minute preparation duties. Chitchatting will help you forget your nerves.
7. Indulge in a nice stiff drink.

IF YOU CLEAN ANYTHING,
CLEAN JUST THESE FIVE SPOTS

1. Corners. Nothing's worse than dust bunnies crashing your party.
2. Kitchen appliances. Focus on the stovetop and refrigerator handle—by the end of your party prep, it will be pretty dingy.
3. Door frames. People tend to hang out in these at parties. Give them a good once-over.
4. All wood surfaces, such as coffee and dining tables.
5. Anything at eye level (check the walls for smudges).

CHERYL'S TEATIME TIPS

1. When using tea bags, remove the paper tags so they don't drop into the pot. I always think they give tea a papery taste, and I wonder if the dyes from the tags seep into the brew.

2. If you get an annoying tea stain on your favorite tablecloth, use this time-tested trick: Pour sugar into a quart of water until the sugar no longer dissolves. Immerse the linen in the solution for a few minutes and rinse with warm water.

3. Store tea (whether loose or bagged) in an airtight container to retain freshness and fragrance.

4. When making tea for a crowd (about forty or fifty guests), I like to create a strong, concentrated brew beforehand and then just pour a couple of tablespoons or so in each person's cup followed by hot water. That way, everyone can adjust the strength to their liking. To make the concentrate, bring 1½ quarts of water to a boil, add ¼-pound loose tea, let steep about five minutes, then pour into a teapot.

MAKE YOUR OWN TEA BLEND

It's so much fun to experiment with different herbs to find flavors that you truly love. Here's a basic formula to follow: Combine flowery herbs like chamomile or dandelion petals with a fruity flavor like raspberry and a cooling herb like peppermint. And think outside the box: Herbs not commonly known for tea can be delicious—and healthy. In the olden days, sage was known as a terrific medicinal herb; for an excellent sore-throat remedy, add 2 teaspoons fresh sage leaves to boiling water, strain after 10 minutes. And if you're lucky enough to have rose bushes, pick those rose hips! They're at their most vitamin-packed in the fall. Just allow them to dry for a week (place them on a tray covered with a clean cloth) before brewing.

SERVE TASTY, HEALTHY, FANCY-FREE FOOD

Nutritious yet delicious—that's the key to this menu. Set dishes out on a buffet so guests can help themselves. A starter of creamy broccoli puree feels decadent; easy-to-prepare wilted greens with tomatoes and pistachios looks gourmet. Follow these with a soul-satisfying and protein-rich main course of bison with tomatoes and pomegranate seeds, paired with herb-roasted sweet potatoes and yams. Then end the meal with a liquid palate cleanser—peppermint tea served in Asian teacups.

ROASTED SWEET POTATOES & YAMS WITH FRESH HERBS

Serves 10 Prep time: 15 minutes Total time: 1 hour 30 minutes

Ingredients:

3 large garnet yams or
　3 large sweet potatoes
½ cup extra-virgin olive oil
¼ cup freshly squeezed lemon juice

⅛ to ¼ teaspoon cayenne pepper
　(if you like spicy, use ¼ teaspoon)
½ teaspoon kosher salt
½ teaspoon freshly ground black pepper
¼ cup chopped fresh chives

Directions:

1. Preheat the oven to 375°F. Line two baking sheets with aluminum foil. **2.** Cut the sweet potatoes lengthwise into 1-inch-thick wedges. **3.** In a large bowl, combine the oil, lemon juice, and cayenne. Toss the sweet potatoes in the mixture until well coated. Place on the prepared baking sheets and spread the sweet potatoes out evenly. Bake for 45 minutes. Sprinkle with salt and black pepper and half of the chives, toss, and continue to roast for 20 to 30 minutes longer, until the thickest wedges are soft. **4.** Let cool slightly, then garnish with the remaining chives. Serve warm.

CREAMY BROCCOLI PUREE

Serves 10 Prep time: 25 minutes Total time: 1 hour

Ingredients:

½ cup (1 stick) unsalted butter
　or Nature's Balance
2 shallots, chopped
4 cloves garlic, peeled and coarsely
　chopped
1 medium onion, peeled and chopped
2 chiles de arbol, sliced
1 tablespoon fresh thyme leaves
2 bay leaves

2 large russet potatoes, chopped
2 pounds broccoli (frozen or fresh),
　florets and stems, chopped
6 cups vegetable or chicken stock
2 teaspoons kosher salt, or more to taste
1 teaspoon ground white pepper
½ teaspoon ground coriander
Garlic chips, grated Parmesan,
　or fresh chives

Directions:

1. In a large pot, melt the butter over medium heat. Add the shallots, garlic, onion, chiles, thyme, and bay leaves and sauté until the onion is translucent. **2.** Add the potatoes and broccoli and cook for 10 minutes. **3.** Add the stock, salt, and white pepper and bring to a boil, then reduce the heat and cook at a simmer until the vegetables are tender, about 20 minutes. **4.** Remove from the heat and discard the bay leaves. Working in batches, puree the soup until smooth in a blender or food processor. **5.** Return the puree to the pot and season to taste with salt and black pepper. Stir in the coriander. Simmer over low heat until ready to serve. Garnish with garlic chips, cheese, or chives.

CABBAGE CENTERPIECES

You'll need:
* Purple cabbage
* Sharp paring knife
* Shallow bowl

1. Wash the cabbage well. 2. Peel off any layers that look tired or worn. 3. Slice a piece off the bottom so that the cabbage sits flat in a bowl of water. You can also use a cabbage as a vase itself by hollowing it out: Cut a square hole in the top of the cabbage with a sharp paring knife. Tuck a piece of floral foam into the hole, and pour water on top to saturate. Then stick pretty flowers inside (cut stems at a sharp angle so that they pierce the floral foam). Purple flowers like sweet pea look especially gorgeous.

Party Highlights

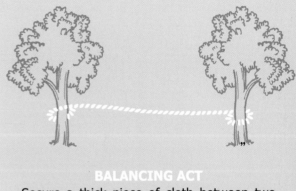

BALANCING ACT

Secure a thick piece of cloth between two trees about a foot off the ground and above soft ground (you could also use a mound of sand). Ask guests to kick off their shoes and try walking across the line. The idea is that the harder you try to balance, the harder it is to stay on course. So you have to essentially "let go" to not fall off.

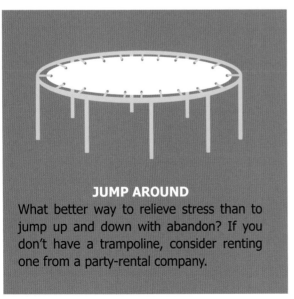

JUMP AROUND

What better way to relieve stress than to jump up and down with abandon? If you don't have a trampoline, consider renting one from a party-rental company.

Happy Accidents

STICKY SITUATION: You're setting up the party and realize you don't have enough chairs.

HOSTESS RECOVERY: No chairs? No problem! Grab a bunch of throw pillows from beds and sofas around the house and toss them on the floor around a coffee table. For a casual party, it sets the vibe, allowing guests to get comfortable and really relax.

STICKY SITUATION: You ordered centerpieces from a florist but when they arrived they weren't exactly what you had in mind—they were too dense and formal, and didn't look right.

HOSTESS RECOVERY: Grab some pruners and head to the garden. Snip plants and tree branches (like magnolia) to tone down the formal centerpieces with an earthier mix. In the future, when planning a party, you'll order simpler—and less expensive—centerpieces knowing you'll spruce them up with pieces from your garden. Voilà—a new cost-saving idea.

FAKE THE MEAL:
Embrace Your Best, and
Resource the Rest

If you're not a huge cook (and trust me, I know the feeling), then don't make the meal yourself. Consider ordering in soup from your favorite restaurant. Some of my favorites for this type of party are lentil soup, barley vegetable soup, mushroom soup, minestrone, carrot ginger, wonton soup, or a great lemongrass soup. Add a fresh garnish and you've got yourself a homemade-looking dish. Then complement the soup with a fruit or vegetable platter from a local deli, plus bowls of wasabi peas or curry cashews. Or get hummus, falafel, and couscous from a great Mediterranean restaurant, and fill a glass drinks dispenser with iced green tea or passion fruit tea.

TWISTS ON A THEME: MORE PARTY IDEAS FROM CHERYLSTYLE.COM

ARRANGE IT!: Bring your girlfriends together for an evening of Ikebana flower arranging. With an origami invitation, set the mood for a relaxing night enjoying spring rolls, edamame, and sake. A furoshiki (Japanese wrapping cloth) with arranging tools graces each place setting. Add haiku and this gathering is for you!

"CAUSE" IT'S RIGHT: Talk about a party that gives back! Invite your guests to not only dine on great food, but also have meaningful conversation around trying to right a wrong in the world. Tie it in with ethnic food and decor, and awareness won't be the only thing you raise.

POTTED!: Connect with the earth's bounty in this buffet-style potluck party where the collected food is served in lined garden pots, and garden tools are used as serving utensils. Colorful seasonal veggies are decorative table additions, and place settings are reminiscent of nurturing botanicals.

Martini Birthday Bash

*For throwing a cocktail party as
chic as the birthday girl herself...*

We've all been to dinner party after dinner party—after a while, they start to feel the same. This party stirs things up. By serving food in martini glasses, you'll give the event a lighthearted and irreverent (it'll be neat, as in martini—get it?) feel that instantly puts guests at ease. It also allows you to cut down on portions, so you can save on expenses. Use lots of candles to give the space a come-hither glow, and go for a luxe mix of textures—pair pewter pitchers (even when tarnished they'll look cool!) with gorgeous crystal candleholders, and glam up the table with oversized martini-glass centerpieces. A shimmering palette of clear, white, and turquoise feels serene and sleek—the perfect complement to that oh-so-sophisticated martini (and birthday girl, of course!).

"I wanted this party to reflect my friend Joy's sparkling personality, so I brought in shimmery flower accents and pops of vivid, can't-miss-it turquoise. Apple martinis—her favorite drink—are sure to raise spirits even more."

"Former NBA pro Eddie Johnson is a superstar when it comes to free throws, but throwing parties? He's a rookie at best. Eddie wanted to plan a birthday party for his wife, Joy, but since she's an event planner herself and is always throwing parties for others, it couldn't be run of the mill. To be truly memorable, it had to scream 'Joy!' So I asked Eddie if Joy had a signature drink, and he told me she loved apple martinis. Bingo. I decided to make this a 'Joytini' party, where we'd serve her favorite drink in pretty hand-painted glasses and a few of her favorite dishes in martini glasses. Joy was definitely shaken up—in a good way."

REFLECT THE JOY

To evoke a hip boutique hotel feel, try to keep the palette understated by mixing clear Lucite and turquoise. On the table, glass plates showcase a bold place mat underneath; you can even print out menu cards and let them peek out from underneath the plates to give guests an idea of the goodies to come. Oversized martini-glass centerpieces feel almost fairy-tale-like; vodka-bottle place cards instantly set a celebratory mood. Use lots of votives in clear glass holders to make the table extra sparkly. If you can host this by a pool, perfect—the palette will tie right in with the water.

ADD A SPLASH

Dress up solid turquoise napkins with a chic adornment. We found glass flowers from zgallerie.com that we wrapped around the napkins; the guests loved them. They took them off and started wearing them as rings and bracelets. You can raid your jewelry box for pretty brooches, or look around flea markets for bargain costume jewelry.

SIP IT, STRAIGHT UP

Pre-pour a bunch of apple martinis before guests arrive so you're not frantically whipping them up on the spot. Give each guest a different martini glass (these are from lolitamartiniglasses.com) to make them feel special—and know which drink is theirs. If you'd rather not shell out the cash for glasses, opt for acrylic ones instead. They're sturdier than standard plastic but still inexpensive.

END THE NIGHT WITH ZEST

I always like to offer a surprise as the party is winding down, just when guests think all the surprises are over. We had Joy's daughter "crash" the party and sing a wonderful rendition of "Happy Birthday." Joy was, well, overjoyed. Other surprises? You can collect keys in a bowl at the beginning of the party to make sure everyone's fit to drive later, and sneakily put a fun key chain (a martini glass, perhaps?) on each key ring as a reminder of the night.

Place bottles of vodka in ice buckets on the table so guests can help themselves.

10 COCKTAIL IDEAS IF YOU DON'T LOVE MARTINIS

1. **Fuzzy Navel:** 1½ ounces peach schnapps topped with orange juice and a cherry.
2. **Greyhound:** 1½ ounces vodka topped with grapefruit juice.
3. **Kamikaze:** 1½ ounces vodka, 1 ounce triple sec, 1 ounce sours mix, ½ ounce lime juice.
4. **Madras:** 1½ ounces vodka topped with equal parts orange and cranberry juice.
5. **Lemon Drop:** 1½ ounces vodka, 1 ounce triple sec, 1 ounce sours mix, ½ ounce fresh lime juice.
6. **Negroni:** ¾ ounce Campari, ¾ ounce gin, ¾ ounce sweet vermouth.
7. **Italian Spritz:** 2 to 3 ounces sparkling wine, 1½ ounces Aperol (an Italian orange liqueur), splash of club soda.
8. **Citrus Fizz:** 1 cup orange seltzer, 1 tablespoon frozen lemonade, ½ tablespoon lemon juice, 1½ ounces lemon or orange vodka.
9. **Aviation:** 1 ounce fresh lemon juice, 2 ounces gin, ½ ounce maraschino liqueur, ¼ teaspoon simple syrup.
10. **Sidecar:** 1½ ounces Cognac, 1 ounce Cointreau, ½ ounce fresh lemon juice—rim the glass with sugar.

ALTERNATIVE MARTINIS

For each of these drinks, fill a cocktail shaker more than halfway with ice, then add ingredients according to the instructions below. Shake well and serve with a smile!

APPLE MARTINI

Add 2 ounces vodka and ½ ounce Sour Apple Pucker. Garnish the glass with a slice of Granny Smith apple.

CHOCOLATINI

Add 2 ounces vodka and 1 ounce Godiva chocolate liqueur. Garnish with chocolate shavings or toss in a Hershey's Kiss. Serve in a glass rimmed with cocoa powder and sugar.

WATERMELON MARTINI

Add ½ ounce fresh lemon juice, 1 ounce Midori melon liqueur, 1 ounce citrus vodka, and ⅓ ounce fresh watermelon juice.

SALT & PEPPER MARTINI

Add ½ ounce vermouth and 2 ounces Absolut Peppar vodka. Serve in a salt-rimmed glass.

COSMOPOLITAN

Add 1½ ounces vodka, ½ ounce Cointreau, ¾ ounce cranberry juice, and ¼ ounce lime juice.

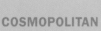

BANANA SPLIT

Add 1 ounce vodka, 1 ounce crème de banana, 1 ounce Godiva white chocolate liqueur, ½ ounce strawberry syrup, ½ ounce heavy cream. Garnish with a strawberry slice.

PLAY WITH YOUR FOOD

Whenever you serve food in unexpected ways, you intrigue guests and make them want to dig right in. At this party, present each course—complete with its own "olive"—in a martini glass. Since the portions are on the smaller side, guests won't feel weighed down.

SHRIMP COCKTAIL

For this course, it's best to use the kind of martini glass that rests in a bed of crushed ice to keep the seafood chilled. Place a dollop of cocktail sauce in the bottom of the glass, and nestle three or four shrimp inside, with the tails facing up to make for easy grabbing. Spear a couple of cherry tomatoes as the "olives."

CHOPPED SALAD

Refreshing chopped veggies drizzled with olive oil and vinegar is the ticket here. When filling up the martini glass, work in layers. I like to put cucumbers in first so they're a nice palate cleanser when you reach the end of the salad. On top, add orange or yellow peppers, red onion, and yellow tomatoes. Spear an olive and your "martini" salad is complete.

FETTUCCINE & MEATBALLS

This presentation makes pasta look homemade (even though you got it from an Italian restaurant). Spoon a tablespoon or so of sauce into the bottom of the martini glass and add one meatball. Then swirl some fettuccine on your fork and carefully ease it into the glass, followed by a little more sauce and one more meatball to act as the "olive."

STRAWBERRY LAYER CAKE

Serves 10
Prep time: 35 minutes
Total time: 1 hour 10 minutes

Ingredients:

For the cake layers:
3 cups all-purpose flour, sifted
3½ teaspoons baking powder
1½ teaspoons kosher salt
2 cups sugar
1 cup (2 sticks) unsalted butter, softened
4 large eggs
2 teaspoons pure vanilla extract
1 cup milk
2 cups sliced strawberries

For the buttercream frosting:
1½ cups (3 sticks) unsalted butter, softened
4½ cups confectioners' sugar
½ teaspoon pure vanilla extract
10 strawberries, sliced, plus
5 whole strawberries for garnish

Directions:

1. Make the cake layers: Preheat the oven to 350°F. Grease and flour two 9-inch round cake pans. **2.** In a medium bowl, combine the flour, baking powder, and salt. **3.** In a separate large bowl, cream together the sugar and butter. Beat in the eggs, one at a time, then stir in the vanilla. Add the flour mixture to the creamed mixture. Stir in the milk until the batter is smooth. Gently fold in the strawberries and pour the batter into the prepared pans. **4.** Bake for 30 to 40 minutes, until the cake springs back to the touch. Let cool completely on wire racks, then loosen the edges and turn out of the pans. **5.** Make the buttercream frosting: In a large bowl, mix the butter and confectioners' sugar with an electric mixer on medium speed until well combined. Increase the speed to medium-high; add the vanilla. Beat until light and fluffy, about 3 minutes more. **6.** Frost the top of the bottom cake layer and cover with the sliced strawberries. Set the second cake layer on top. Frost the entire cake, including the sides. Decorate the top with the whole strawberries.

MARTINI-GLASS CENTERPIECES

1. Buy a few oversized plastic martini glasses (check out decorativenovelty.com and save-on-crafts.com for options), long bamboo skewers, Styrofoam balls (about three or four inches in diameter), and green mums. **2.** Using a bamboo skewer, spear a Styrofoam ball through the center. **3.** Cut the mums' stems a few inches long and at a sharp angle so they can easily pierce the ball. Stick each mum into the ball right next to each other to create a tight cluster of flowers. **4.** Use straight pins to help blooms stay flush with the ball, if necessary. Fill the martini glass halfway with water so that it looks like vodka, rest your skewered mum "olive" on top, and your centerpiece is complete . . . mum's the word!

Party Highlights

BOTTLE CONTEST
See who can flip and catch a bottle the way Tom Cruise did in the movie *Cocktail*. Plastic bottles may be best here!

PICK YOUR POISON
Have the bartender (someone you hired or someone you designate) create a few martinis with a secret ingredient—anything from cassis to ginger to mint. Give guests shot glasses to taste. Whoever guesses the secret ingredient wins a prize.

MARTINI-MAKING CONTEST
Set up a bar with all the accoutrements (gin, vermouth, lemons, limes, olives). Instruct each guest to whip up a classic martini (you can leave a card on the bar with the recipe). Designate one person as the judge—then give him a celebratory cup of coffee afterward!

Happy Accidents

STICKY SITUATION: As you're bringing the strawberry layer cake out from the kitchen, you lose your footing and the cake falls into the lid of the cake dome (thank goodness that was on!).

HOSTESS RECOVERY: Rather than making a big deal of it, you take it all in stride. You say, "Does anyone have a spoon? Get out your spoons, everyone!" and place the now upside-down cake on the table and tell everyone to dig in. Or scoop it out and serve it with a smile and a laugh. This "mishap" actually lightens the mood of the party, gives everyone a good giggle, and leads to a communal dessert that's a lot more fun than eating all prim and proper with your own plate.

TWISTS ON A THEME: MORE PARTY IDEAS FROM CHERYLSTYLE.COM

BRING OUT YOUR INNER HIPPIE: Forget the dining table at this party and seat your guests on throw pillows around a coffee table with a Lazy Susan on top. Ask them to come dressed in tie-dye, and set up four fondue pots: a mild cheese with veggies; a savory fondue like garlic cream cheese or hot crab; a broth-based fondue for dipping chicken and steak; and a dessert fondue like chocolate caramel or mocha cinnamon.

GOOD FORTUNE: This party is all about dim sum and then some—with guests arriving in silk pajamas and enjoying a simple Chinese takeout menu that you transfer to elegant red takeout containers. Trust me, no one will think a thing about it. Custom fortunes you create and tuck inside fortune cookies will leave guests Tso happy.

VINTAGE & VINO: This dinner party is a great way to showcase your collection of antiques—and wines. Set up your home to feel like an antique store. When guests arrive, they'll head to the "Appraisal Bar" for a blind wine tasting. Guests also bring a "collected" place setting to the table and share their stories about it over dinner. The attire? Vintage, of course!

Guys-Only Scotch & Cigars Gathering

*For honoring your favorite guy
in a man-cave environment...*

Face it: Your man doesn't need another tie. What he just might need, though, is some good old-fashioned guy time. This year, give him the run of the house by setting up a boys-only party complete with whiskey, cigars, and hearty grub that lets the men be men and allows you to duck out for girls' night (woo hoo!), or for some special mommy time alone with the kids. You'll be able to prepare food ahead of schedule and not have to deal with serving or socializing, so this event is essentially stress-free. The decor here is boys-will-be-boys, so it's fun to scour your home for found treasures that you can use to decorate the table—whether it's a swatch of leather, flea-market-find flasks, or rustic ornaments you collected on your last vacation. This is truly a party that benefits both parties!

"Cigars, Scotch, leather accents . . . When you put them all together, the effect is truly a man's bastion—a place us girls wouldn't want to be in anyway!"

"For one of my husband's birthday parties, I wasn't into giving him a run-of-the-mill present. I wanted to gift him with more of an experience. So I came up with the idea of a whiskey-and-cigar-fueled man-cave birthday, where I'd arrange the party beforehand and then give them full reign of the house. He has a taste for Scotch, so the theme seemed fitting for him and also something I knew his pals could get behind. I must say, giving your man a night to himself is kind of foolproof—I know we're all wonderful and everything, but what guy wouldn't want that?!"

CATER TO HIS INNER CAVEMAN

Real men don't need plates. Keep the look simple and rustic by repurposing wooden cutting boards as "chargers" topped with rustic bowls. You can mix and match bowls from what you have in the house, or cobble together a set from flea markets or tag sales. Unless you have a dining table you want to protect, keep things simple and casual by going bare rather than using a fussy tablecloth. We used gray linen napkins and wrapped brown penny loafer–shaped ornaments around them for a manly touch. I love finding ornaments on sale after Christmas that fit my party themes—nowadays you can get ornaments all year round on the internet. Small Pottery Barn flasks act as place cards; simple white stickers with guests' names are handwritten (much more personal than a computer printout).

CREATE A MANLY MOOD

Go for dark, rich colors like burgundy, chocolate, and amber, and keep lights low. If you don't have a dimmer in the room, turn off the overheads and flick on a table lamp or two. Get guys in the Scotch-and-cigars mood by cranking up the jazz. For ideas on how to create a funky jazz playlist, see CherylStyle.com/book.

MAKE FOOD HE CAN MANHANDLE

Guys will love picking apart an edible cheese centerpiece. For the main meal, it's all about hearty stick-to-the-ribs comfort food like a yummy pork and white bean stew (to keep it hot until the guys dip into it, put an earthenware crock in a 350-degree oven for an hour, then pour the stew inside). Corn bread cut into bite-sized cubes soaks up the stew—and the Scotch, for that matter.

SMOKE HIM OUT

Crack a window to circulate air around the room. If your guy is a regular cigar smoker, consider investing in an air purifier—just make sure to get a model with replaceable filters rather than permanent ones; the fibers in permanent filters may disperse odors back into the room over time. If there are any lingering odors after the party, spray the upholstery, curtains, rugs, (even your man's hair if you have to) with an odor eliminator specifically designed to tackle smoke, like GoneSmoke (gonesmoke.com). If you hate the smell of smoke (like I do, quite frankly), you can designate a smoking section outdoors or in your garage. Make leaving the cave appealing to your men by outfitting the area with a few cozy chairs. Consider renting a heat lamp if it's cold where you live (call local party supply companies). And make sure to have plenty of ashtrays on hand so that you don't come home to find cigar butts in your begonias.

Left to right: Scotch on the rocks is sure to make your man smile; a shoe ornament gets repurposed as a napkin treatment.

THE INCREDIBLE, EDIBLE CENTERPIECE

Having the food essentially act as table decor- ation offers a nice guy-friendly alternative to typical flowers. When setting up your cheese centerpiece, you'll want to use different heights to create a sense of abundance and accessibility; this allows people to be at dif- ferent parts of the arrangement simultane- ously so that they don't bump into each other trying to snag a slice of Brie. Look around the house for items you can use to create height, like cigar boxes (used flat or on their sides), pretty vintage-looking books, or antique flasks and flea-market-find mini briefcase ornaments, as shown here. As for arranging the cheese, just try not to let them touch— allow enough space that each variety has its own little *fromage* universe.

WHICH CHEESE TO CHOOSE?

Avoid really stinky cheese for this party; to me, only the people eating the stinky cheese should buy the stinky cheese. It's just not right any other way. Stick to crowd-pleasing favorites like whole-milk mozzarella, a nice goat cheese, and a decadent triple crème—that's always a star. Include a mixture of hard cheeses like aged cheddar or Gouda with softer cheeses like bleu, and try to have an eye-pleasing variety of textures and colors. Next, add in some sweet bites, like dried apricots or peaches, dates, and guava paste (just set it on a small dish), along with savory elements, such as walnuts, Marcona almonds, prosciutto, soppressa, and olives. It would be quite the horror to run out of cheese, so stock up accordingly: figure that you should buy at least a half pound of cheese per person. Take cheese out of the fridge about a half hour before guests arrive—cheese tastes best at room temperature; if it's too cold it loses flavor and texture.

HOW TO SERVE CHEESE

" When I was traveling in France one year, I learned how to avoid chunks of cheese looking unap- petizing once a few people get into it. The idea is to maintain the shape of the cheese. If it's rectangular, slice pieces off one of the short ends, keeping the rectangle intact. If it's triangular, don't just chop off the tip like a brute—slice down one side so that it still looks like a triangle. With a circle, cut it like you're cut- ting into an apple pie. "

Serves 10
Prep time: 30 minutes
Total time: 3 hours, plus 8 hours for soaking beans

Ingredients:

1 pound dried white beans such as cannellini or Great Northern
2 tablespoons olive oil
5 cloves garlic, diced
1 large yellow onion, diced
6 ribs celery, diced
3 chiles de arbol, thinly sliced
¼ cup chopped fresh oregano
¼ cup chopped fresh thyme
¼ cup chopped fresh flat-leaf parsley
10 cups chicken stock
4 pounds smoked ham hocks, or shanks cut into 2-inch pieces
1 pound fresh spinach
Kosher salt and freshly ground black pepper, to taste
Tabasco sauce (optional)

Directions:

1. Pick through the beans and discard any small stones or debris. Rinse well and put the beans in a large bowl with cold water to cover by 3 inches, cover, and set aside at room temperature for 8 hours or overnight. Drain well. 2. In a large pot, warm the oil over medium-high heat. Sauté the garlic, onion, and celery until soft. Add the soaked beans, chiles, oregano, thyme, and parsley and sauté for 15 minutes, stirring frequently. Add the stock and ham hocks and cover the pot. Simmer for 2 to 2¼ hours, until the meat can be easily pulled from the bones and the beans are tender. 3. Just before serving, stir in the spinach and heat through. Add salt and black pepper to taste. Serve with Tabasco sauce, if desired.

10 MORE DELICIOUS
DIG-RIGHT-IN ONE-POT MEALS

1. Arroz con pollo
2. Sloppy Joes
3. Chicken cacciatore
4. Jambalaya
5. Turkey chili
6. Beef stew
7. Chicken tortilla soup
8. Shepherd's pie
9. Sausage gumbo
10. Tuna casserole

Serves 8

For those who don't like Scotch on the rocks, or to help newcomers to whiskey ease into the taste, whip up a Rusty Nail. This two-liquor cocktail (who needs a mixer?) includes honey-sweet Drambuie to tone down the biting Scotch. Blended Scotch (like Johnnie Walker) is typically better for mixed drinks than single malts.

Directions:

1. Pour 12 ounces Scotch into a pitcher, followed by 4 ounces Drambuie, and stir well. Don't put ice in yet, because you don't want to water down your concoction. **2.** When it's time to serve, pour the mixture into rocks glasses filled with ice cubes (crushed ice will melt faster). **3.** You can also strain it into a glass for a Straight Up Nail.

RAISE YOUR SPIRITS: TURN IT INTO A SCOTCH TASTING

To make the party more of a formal tasting:
Set up the Scotch in a separate room from the food—serious Scotch drinkers would have only water and some crackers around to cleanse the palate.

Organize the tasting one of these three ways:

1. SINGLE MALT TASTING: Single malts tend to offer a more distinct taste than, say, blended Scotches. You'd select one Scotch from each of the six main Scotch-producing regions: Islay, the Lowlands, Speyside, the Highlands, Campbeltown, and Islands.

2. VERTICAL TASTING: Sampling different ages from the same brand, like Glenlivet.

3. REGIONAL TASTING: Trying a few Scotches from the same region, like Islay or Speyside.

Once you decide which kind of tasting to host, ask the salesperson at the liquor store to suggest four to five bottles. Just make certain you give him the budget—some Scotches can get pricey.

SCOTCH TASTING
5
IN FIVE STEPS

You can instruct your guy on a few rules and have him teach the crowd later, or print out some guidelines and leave them on a piece of paper on the table.

1: LOOK at the color by holding the glass up to something white, like a piece of paper. Is it pale gold or deep amber?

2: POUR a few drops of bottled water into the Scotch to "open it up" a bit and release the flavors. Don't use tap water—it may contain chlorine that'll alter the taste of the Scotch.

3: SNIFF the Scotch to pick up its scent, whether it's vanilla, caramel, a floral or spicy note, or an earthiness like peat.

4: SIP the Scotch, swish it around, and let it roll over your tongue. Pay attention to how it feels: Is it smooth, oily, dry? Sweet, salty, sour, bitter? Is it warming or does it burn? What flavors come to mind: honey, citrus, chocolate, wood, grass?

5: SWALLOW and note if the flavor immediately goes away, lingers, or changes afterward (called the "finish").

TIP: At each place setting, include a small pad of paper so guests can jot down notes like the name of the Scotch, age, color, nose, palate, and finish.

SOME SCOTCH TRIVIA: What's the difference between Scotch and whiskey? In a nutshell, Scotch is whiskey but not all whiskey is Scotch. Only whiskey made in Scotland can be called Scotch.

HAVANA NICE DAY: THE ART OF SELECTING STOGIES

A cigar shop can be intimidating—hundreds if not thousands of those little guys lined up in rows. Ask the salesperson for help—most times they'll be delighted to assist you. In general, stick to well-known manufacturers, like CAO Gold from Nicaragua (about $4 a cigar) or Sancho Panza from Honduras (about $3.75 each). You can also buy cigars online, and find great deals, on sites like famous-smoke.com or cigarsinternational .com. Just make certain they are shipped properly to avoid them drying out in transit.

Here are some things to know:

- Gently squeeze the cigar up and down the body (rolling it can damage the wrapper). It should feel full and lump-free, and have some give to it without being spongy.
- Inspect the wrapper—it should be smooth and tight, with no dents, major discoloration, or cracks (that means it's dry).
- Look at the exposed tobacco on the side you light (called the foot)—minor discolorations are OK, but you don't want extreme changes in color; this can mean an inferior leaf was used, which may result in uneven burning or an off taste.
- While you're at the store, buy a guillotine cutter to snip the stogie; you place the tip of the cigar inside and the blade slices off the tip prior to smoking.

Happy Accidents

STICKY SITUATION: You flick on the lights in the man-cave room to find that the main overhead light is out...and you have no replacement bulbs.

HOSTESS RECOVERY: Scour the house for candles, grab as many as you can, and scatter them around the room. Now the space is actually cozier and not as glaring, and decidedly more cave-like.

STICKY SITUATION: You set out a bucket of beer for when the guys want a break from the Scotch, but thinking the bottles had twist-off caps, you didn't include the opener.

HOSTESS RECOVERY: The guys made do with ease. They started bragging and showing each other their patented tricks for opening a beer bottle: using a lighter; using a cap from another bottle; using a car key; using a belt buckle. The man-cave testosterone fest was in full force.

TWISTS ON A THEME: MORE PARTY IDEAS FROM CHERYLSTYLE.COM

5-CARD STUDS: Serve a selection of beers from countries around the world, plus big pretzels and various types of mustard for dipping. Each plate holds a shirt "cuff" tucked with a napkin and a playing card to look like an ace up the sleeve. Add poker chips and you have a way for everyone to ante up for some fun.

A COOLER TAILGATE: Join your buddies to cheer on your favorite team while sitting around the MVP—that's right, the cooler! It's the center of attention at this tailgate party. Using a cooler coozie, dress up your cooler with team spirit wear so that the team spirit is one with the distilled "spirits."

SOUP'ER BOWL: This guy-friendly party features soup on the stove and oversized soup bowls wrapped in team beanies to keep them warm and ready to go when the guys are in the mood to eat. Serve a variety of cheese and crackers as accompaniments and this party will be everything the Super Bowl is cracked up to be.

Tween Spa Birthday

*For a pampering, "grown up" party that
both kids and parents will enjoy...*

It's not easy being a tween. They're interesting little people—old enough to exert their opinions but young enough that they still want your input. Seriously, they actually do want you around to a certain extent. (I know it sounds crazy, but it's true—I've been there.) But their ideas for a rocking party might not jibe with yours. Case in point: Your daughter might want to host a dance with boys and girls in her grade, but trust me, boys at that age are not into dancing with them, and they'll end up disappointed. Better to do an all-girl affair—and make it a little grown up with a relaxing spa theme. Here's some ohm-spiration.

"Tween glamour here we come! 'Gems' for blinging flip-flops and sparkly touches feel decadent. What better way to make girls feel like grown-ups for the day?"

"I created this party for one of my tween-age daughters and it was a hit. It allowed her to be showered with attention but still do adult things like get manicures and facials. By acting as manicurist and facialist, I was able to keep an eye on the gang without being too invasive. And she could hang with the girls and chitchat. The result? Pure bliss."

RALLY THE TROOPS

Call around to see if any other moms will volunteer to help you perform manicures and facials. If no one bites, you can always ask a teenager to come over for a few hours—they love to help!

DESIGN A SPA PARADISE

Set up a scene that'll make the girls ooh and aah. Prop Adirondack chairs or chaise longues with comfy throw pillows. Place foot soaks in plastic bins decorated with flower stickers and filled with warm water, a few drops of dishwashing liquid, and pink rose petals in front of each seat. For a touch of glamour, casually drape pink gauzy fabric from poles placed around the seating arrangement, or around tree branches, the way you would on a canopy bed.

SET A SOOTHING MOOD

Scatter aromatherapy candles and lavender potpourri or lavender essential oil in small bowls around the space, and play nature sounds, like that of a rippling river or chirping birds (see CherylStyle.com/book for a relaxing playlist). You can also set up mini Zen fountains.

GIVE THEM THE ROYAL TREATMENT

When guests arrive, hand out pretty-in-pink towel wraps, headbands, and flip-flops, which they'll decorate later. Pamper the girls with manicures, foot soaks, and a choice of either a banana or an avocado face mask.

OFFER HEALTHY, FEEL-GOOD NIBBLES

Serve up healthy snacks like veggie wraps; flower-shaped PB&J sandwiches; water infused with cucumbers, citrus, and mint; and (OK, this one's not particularly healthy, but I couldn't resist) bakery-bought pink cupcakes decorated with beautiful edible flowers. Tiered trays on side tables are perfect for this party. They'll make the girls feel special as they pick a goody from a tier—plus, they just look abundant and adorable.

SEND THEM OFF WITH A GIRLY GIFT

This is a great way to cater to the young girl in all of them. Fill a basket with spa supplies like nail files, nail stickers, polish, and bath bombs and add a cute spa teddy bear—you can deck out your own with robes and headbands or buy the bears from a website. You'll find the bears I used on Amazon.com (look up "spa teddy bear").

Clockwise from top left: Tiered platters make cupcakes feel like little gems; a spa teddy bear is a sweet, cuddly take-home gift; soaking toes in rose-petal foot baths; blinging flip-flops caters to fashionistas-to-be. Opposite: Adirondack chairs propped with comfy pillows set the pampering scene.

Directions:

Buy pink cupcakes from a bakery and spruce them up to look home-made. You can "repot" them into pretty pink cupcake holders—I found ones with ruffles on them that I just couldn't resist. Then decorate the tops with edible flowers. You can usually find these in the herb section of the supermarket or at a farmers' market or nursery.

INFUSED WATER

Directions:

A refreshing alternative to sugar-laden juice, infused water looks amazing in clear glass vessels. All you need to do is cut up slices of your favorite fruits or herbs, toss in a large drink dispenser (you can also use pitchers), fill to the top with cold water, and let sit for two hours. About 10 minutes before guests arrive, top each canister with a healthy amount of ice. Have fun with your infusions. I love the simplicity of cucumber water and mint water. But for gorgeous color and a really nice medley of flavors, I also like to create a citrus brew with lemons, limes, and grapefruit. If you want something even more surprising, consider mixing herbs and fruits in one canister. Try out lavender-lemon, watermelon-basil, and pineapple-mint.

This luscious smoothie, indulgent and healthy, offers the best of both worlds. All the wonderful health benefits of strawberries are magnified when paired with avocado. Strawberries just met their match! This recipe is easily doubled for larger parties; just blend it in batches.

Serves 4
Prep time: 15 minutes
Total time: 15 minutes

Ingredients:
1 cup low-fat strawberry yogurt
1 cup low-fat milk
1 to 2 cups ice
½ avocado
2 cups strawberries, hulled and halved, plus extra for garnish

Directions:
1. In a blender, combine the yogurt, milk, ice, avocado, and strawberries. Blend on high speed until creamy and smooth. **2.** Pour into individual glasses and garnish with the extra strawberries. Serve cold. Can be prepared up to six hours ahead of time and chilled in the refrigerator.

VEGGIE WRAPS

Directions:

Perfect for a light young ladies' lunch. To make them, look for the thinnest wraps you can find—thick ones are harder to stay together when rolled. You can get plain wraps or spinach or tomato ones for a pretty color pop. Buy a head of romaine, peel off nice long slices, and wash and dry well. Cut veggies (you can use any you like, but I love carrots, cucumbers, and avocado) into long strips. Spread cream cheese on each wrap, place a piece of lettuce on top, then fill with a handful of veggies. Roll like a burrito by folding up the bottom first and then folding in the sides before rolling and spearing with a few toothpicks. Using a sharp serrated knife, cut into four or five slices. I like to add a piece of a pink boa feather on top for pizzazz.

5 OTHER DECEPTIVELY HEALTHY SNACK IDEAS

Looking for more healthy snacks? Your tweens will love these (and never be the wiser).

1. Create a snack mix with various kinds of nuts, dried fruit, and cereal.
2. Top cucumber slices with tuna salad.
3. Dip bananas in low-fat chocolate syrup and freeze for a fruity ice-pop treat.
4. Make fruit kebabs (think bananas, melon, and apples) and serve with a blueberry-yogurt dip.
5. Top whole wheat crackers with peanut butter, drizzled honey, and strawberry slices.

MAKE YOUR OWN LOTION

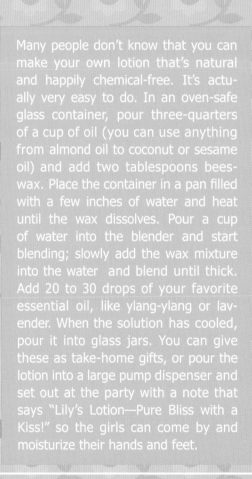

Many people don't know that you can make your own lotion that's natural and happily chemical-free. It's actually very easy to do. In an oven-safe glass container, pour three-quarters of a cup of oil (you can use anything from almond oil to coconut or sesame oil) and add two tablespoons beeswax. Place the container in a pan filled with a few inches of water and heat until the wax dissolves. Pour a cup of water into the blender and start blending; slowly add the wax mixture into the water and blend until thick. Add 20 to 30 drops of your favorite essential oil, like ylang-ylang or lavender. When the solution has cooled, pour it into glass jars. You can give these as take-home gifts, or pour the lotion into a large pump dispenser and set out at the party with a note that says "Lily's Lotion—Pure Bliss with a Kiss!" so the girls can come by and moisturize their hands and feet.

HOMEMADE AVOCADO MASKS

Why spend a lot of money on store-bought masks when you can make your own from fresh ingredients? Here's how:

1. Buy one avocado per guest. 2. Carve out the avocado meat and place in a large metal bowl (to keep the mixture cold). 3. Add a few squirts of fresh lemon to keep the avocado from turning brown. 4. With a fork or potato masher, blend until creamy. That's all it takes—super easy and hydrating!

Party Highlights

SPIN THE NAIL POLISH

I love this game—and the girls will love it too. Put all the nail polish in a pail or big bowl and have the girls sit in a circle on the ground. Instruct the birthday girl to pick a nail polish color, put it in the middle of the circle, and spin. Whoever it lands on has to paint one toe that color; then she picks a different color and spins. At the end of the game, you'll have a wacky array of feet walking around, let me tell you.

BLINGED-OUT FLIP-FLOPS

What tween doesn't want some bling? Have the girls create one-of-a-kind super cool footwear that they can show off. Buy an array of rhinestones and plastic gems in various colors, and set them in bowls. Put out craft glue (or low-heat glue guns with supervision) and cotton swabs. After the masterpieces are done, let sit for at least 20 minutes so the bling can set. This is best on a low table with throw pillows around it so the girls can sit or kneel.

EMBRACE YOUR BEST, RESOURCE THE REST

Rather than cooking, you can always buy a veggie platter and set out various store-bought dips like hummus, onion dip, and yogurt with dill. Order in turkey wraps from a local deli, and serve strawberries on skewers—decadence!

MANICURE MANIA

On a side table, set out a variety of nail polish colors, and have tools like cotton swabs and cotton balls on hand, plus nail polish remover, files, buffers, and nail stickers for customization. If there are more girls than moms able to give manicures, put out a clipboard and sign-up sheet so the guests can secure a time slot.

HAIR STATION

Set up a table with curling irons, blow-dryers, and flat irons (if you're hosting the party outside you'll need an extension cord or outdoor outlet for these), mousse, hair spray, brushes, and a variety of barrettes, clips, and hair ties. Let the girls go wild by giving each other fun new hairdos. Have a few disposable cameras on hand so the girls can take pictures.

Happy Accidents

STICKY SITUATION: The spa honoree wakes up sick the morning of her party—and guests are already on their way.

HOSTESS RECOVERY: Bring the party to her! When all the guests have arrived, tell them that the guest of honor is not feeling "in the pink" today. But make the most of it. Pass out pink postcards and have each of them write a get-well wish. Then, take groups of three into her bedroom with their cards and a flower to add to a vase for a pretty bouquet. After a brief visit with friends, Mom can give the birthday girl a manicure and a special back rub, and carry on with the party outside (ask another mom to help). Her friends will have made an extra-special connection with her that she'll always remember.

TWISTS ON A THEME: MORE PARTY IDEAS FROM CHERYLSTYLE.COM

PAINT-BY-NUMBER SLUMBER: This fun slumber party features fabric painting onto girly tees that become sleepwear. The dining and craft tables are set up with wood palettes as place mats, and finger foods are dipped into colorful sauces squeezed from paint tubes. (New empty tubes can be found at any art-supply store.) Make-it-yourself ice cream sundaes will be their masterpieces!

ETIQUETTE WITH DECADENCE: Learn the rules of etiquette while blinging with your BFFs! Glue sparkles onto plastic dishes and flatware—then set the table "properly" using a place mat from CherylStyle.com/book. Enjoy giggles while reading the "What Not to Do at the Dinner Table" cards.

SECRET INGREDIENT: Take the party girls into the kitchen with aprons and chef's hats. Help them make individual potpies and corn bread, and decorate cupcakes. The delight continues when they sit down at the table and find their napkin has a whisk attached, their plate is a pie tin, and their drinking glass is a measuring cup.

Meet & Potatoes Dinner Party

For extra-special guests, from your boss
to your mother-in-law...

Boss coming to dinner? Hosting an out-of-town client—or long-lost relatives? Don't panic. Here's a foolproof way to lighten the mood and put people at ease. Rather than the traditional (and sometimes off-putting) crystal-and-china affair, this party is chic but casual, with comfort-food classics, rustic spud-inspired centerpieces, and engaging place settings that spark conversation. This twist on the usual way of setting a table isn't just for guests, mind you. It's also for you—it makes creating what's supposed to be a fancy and everything-in-its-place affair more spirited. You can have fun with the process by mixing and matching seemingly disparate elements rather than having to set the table with all that formal china you got on your wedding day. And when you're relaxed and happy, so are your guests—it's contagious. Bring on the bigwigs!

"Rustic burlap and potatoes that look like they were plucked right from the earth create a gorgeous creative juxtaposition when paired with sleek plates, crystal, and crinkly silk napkins."

"When my friend asked me to help her throw a dinner party for her husband's clients and a few colleagues, she wanted to go all-out formal. At her urging, we set the table with sparkling crystal, fine china, and long-stemmed red roses. Ick. It just didn't feel right—the formal table conveyed that we had to sit properly and behave ourselves. It was way too sterile. So I changed the focus and decided to give this party a name. I came up with a twist on Meet and Greet and created Meet and Potatoes. Off went the crisp white tablecloth. Instead, I left the wood table naked—it felt more comforting this way—then used raw-cut burlap as table runners. I left some of the crystal on the table (wineglasses, candlesticks) but swapped out the water goblets for casual everyday ones and replaced fancy china chargers for rustic rattan. Ah, much better."

SPARK CONVERSATION

Use name cards as conversation starters. Come up with unexpected potato-puns for each person's name (think Larry Lyonnaise, Steven Spud, Betsy Baked), and on the back of the cards include a spud-related trivia question, like: Where was the potato chip invented? (Answers can go below the question.) This serves multiple functions: It keeps guests occupied, taking the pressure off you in case you need to slip away from the table. Plus, instead of talking about the weather, conversation will quickly turn to rippled versus flat and the latest baked-potato-chip variety— lighthearted chitchat rather than the traditional get-to-know-yous.

MASH-UP COLORS AND TEXTURES

Focus on cream and tan, with hits of spunky chartreuse, to energize the room. Mixing rough with shiny, soft with sleek feels earthy and calming, and not at all intimidating. The wooden table, rattan chargers, and touches of burlap bring the stuffy china and crystal glasses down to earth, but the table still conveys "You are important to me."

KEEP IT CASUAL WITH CANDLES

Flickering candlelight makes a formal dining room seem friendlier. When decorating with candles, stick to one color (I prefer off-white) so the effect is chic, not chaotic. Candles on a shiny wood table are especially nice because they'll look even more reflective. When placing candlesticks around the table, think in groupings of three. Vary heights so you have one tall, one squat, and one medium—it's more visually interesting this way, and allows the eye to move around the table. Candlesticks don't have to match exactly, but keep to a common theme, like crystal in different shapes or cut designs.

CREATE A SMART SEATING CHART

Although I didn't do it at this party, often I love putting women on one end and men on the other, rather than boy-girl, because the men end up talking over the women, and someone could be left sitting there in silence. I'll even break up couples, and if anyone balks, I'll say, "C'mon, you don't want to be in the middle of us talking, do you?" Usually that does the trick. Try to seat quiet types next to your more talkative guests, and keep those argumentative types (if you know who they are) at opposite ends.

USE THESE T.I.P.S FOR ENTERTAINING V.I.P.S

When you're meeting people for the first time, it can be tough to remember names. Think of how it makes you feel when you know someone you're talking to has no idea what your name is. It just makes you feel a little...less special.

HERE ARE SOME TRICKS FOR REMEMBERING PEOPLE'S NAMES:

- Repeat the name. When you're introduced, say, "So nice to meet you, Jason."

- Think of something that rhymes with the person's name, like Paul Ball or Kelly Belly.

- Create a mental picture of this person standing next to a celebrity or someone else you know who has the same name.

Below: Potato place settings are sure to spark conversation. Opposite: Pour your wine into small glass cups instead of the usual stemware.

TAKE YOUR TABLE SETTING
FROM FANCY TO FABULOUS

MAKE CRUSHED SILK NAPKINS

This idea, seen at left, comes from designer Ann Gish. I've always loved how she uses a fancy material in a toned-down, casual way. It's genius.

1. Run silk napkins under cool water until thoroughly saturated. Squeeze out excess water.

2. Twist each napkin, then fold it over itself and put a rubber band at the bottom to secure.

3. When dry, take the rubber band off and you'll have a nice crinkly piece of art. To further the rustic charm, place a piece of burlap on top and secure with raffia.

RETHINK YOUR CENTERPIECES

1. Fill small bushels with bright-green Granny Smith apples.

2. Grab four or five empty wine bottles, scrub off the labels (or not), and fill with sprigs of ivy or other trailing plants.

3. Adorn mismatched glass vases with playful, colorful pinwheels.

4. Lay down a rich-colored table runner (think aubergine or terra-cotta) and toss pretty dried leaves or dried flowers on top.

LIVEN UP THOSE LINENS

1. Scour post-holiday sales to find inexpensive ornaments to tie around napkins. Guests can take them home as a reminder of the night.

2. Give each setting a different colorful hair band (fresh from the drugstore, of course).

3. Tie with a pretty grosgrain ribbon and let the ends hang loose.

4. Secure with a piece of raffia, then tuck in a wildflower.

5. Tie on a licorice string for a sweet surprise.

6. Use a shiny tassel.

MIX AND MATCH YOUR DISHES

1. Top round placemats with square dishes for a geometric punch.

2. Place a lacy place mat (or any kind with cutouts) over a bold tablecloth so you can see the color through the design.

3. Combine ornate flea-market-find floral dishes with solid-colored chargers.

4. Pair bold-colored dishes, like hot pink or cobalt, with rustic pewter chargers.

5. Mix matte ceramic dishes with high-gloss lacquer ones.

Serves 10
Prep time: 15 minutes
Total time: 15 minutes

Ingredients:

4 cups fresh flat-leaf parsley

2 cups fresh mint

2 tablespoons fresh thyme

3 cloves garlic

2 dried chiles de arbol

4 anchovies

Juice of 1 lemon

¼ teaspoon kosher salt

1½ cups extra-virgin olive oil

Directions:

1. In a food processor, pulse the parsley, mint, thyme, garlic, chiles, anchovies, lemon juice, and salt until a smooth paste forms. **2.** Slowly add the oil and process until smooth, about 1 minute. Transfer to an airtight container and refrigerate until ready to use, up to 6 hours. Bring to room temperature before serving.

Serves 10
Prep time: 1 hour
Total time: 2 hours 30 minutes, plus 8 hours for marinating

Ingredients:
1 whole filet of beef (5 to 6 pounds trimmed)
½ cup fresh flat-leaf parsley leaves
2 dried chiles de arbol, minced
3 cloves garlic
1 tablespoon kosher salt
1 tablespoon freshly ground black pepper
Olive oil

Directions:

1. Trim the meat of all excess fat and silverskin. Tie with kitchen string at 2-inch intervals, tucking the thinner portion underneath so it will cook evenly. **2.** In a food processor, pulse together the parsley, chiles, and garlic until finely minced. Rub the meat with the mixture, wrap in plastic wrap, and refrigerate for 8 hours or overnight. **3.** One hour prior to cooking, remove the meat from the refrigerator and let rest at room temperature; 20 minutes before cooking, sprinkle all over with the salt and black pepper. **4.** Preheat the oven to 400°F. **5.** Heat a heavy-duty roasting pan over high heat for 2 minutes, then add enough oil to just cover the bottom of the pan; heat until the oil begins to smoke. **6.** Pat the meat dry and place it in the pan; cook undisturbed for about 4 minutes, until the bottom is a rich brown. Turn the beef and sear until all sides are browned, about 4 minutes on each side. **7.** Put a rack in the roasting pan, put the meat on the rack, and roast until the internal temperature reaches 125°F for medium-rare, about 25 minutes. (Check the temperature after 15 minutes; the roasting time will vary depending on the searing time.) Remove from the oven and let the meat rest in a warm spot for at least 15 minutes before slicing. Serve warm.

Ingredients:

1 teaspoon each garlic powder, black pepper, fresh dill, and salt
Extra-virgin olive oil
2 pounds red potatoes, cut into wedges

Directions:

1. Preheat oven to 400°F. **2.** In a small bowl, mix together spices. **3.** Pour olive oil into a large bowl, add potatoes and spices, coating thoroughly. **4.** Line a baking sheet with aluminum foil and place potatoes on top. **5.** Bake for about 40 minutes.

EASY VEGETARIAN ENTRÉE OPTIONS
(that even your carnivore friends will love)

1. **Eggplant Rollatini:** A healthy pasta dish.
2. **Bean and Cheese Enchiladas:** Cheesy heaven.
3. **Pasta Primavera:** Stick to angel hair for a not-too-heavy meal.
4. **Vegetarian Chili:** Comfort food at its best.
5. **Cabbage Lasagna:** Using chopped cabbage instead of pasta makes this dish so light.
6. **Sweet Potato Casserole:** Stick-to-the-ribs goodness.
7. **Asparagus Risotto:** Who doesn't like risotto?
8. **Polenta-Stuffed Peppers:** Delicious and nutritious!
9. **Vegetable Alphabet Soup:** Toss some potatoes in there to make it extra hearty.
10. **Moussaka** (with mushrooms instead of meat): Rich and lovely.

FOODS I NEVER SERVE AT A SIT-DOWN DINNER (AND WHY)

Corn and quinoa. They get stuck in your teeth. Not a good look.

Lobster and crab. Just messy, and no one really knows what to do with the shells.

Same goes for oysters. If you don't know to turn your shell over after you slurp up your little guy, you leave your dish a disaster for the rest of us to look at!

Stringy cheese. It's really hard to wrestle the cheese while trying to carry on a conversation.

Truffle oil. You'll get a love-it-or-hate-it reaction from people. So really know your guests before you include this flavor.

Exotic things no one knows what to do with, like a whole fish. When I see something staring back at me, I lose my appetite. It might seem like fancy fare, but you run the risk of turning stomachs.

WINES OF THE TIMES

Contrary to popular belief, there's no rule that you must drink red wine with red meat—it's really a personal preference. So be prepared with both red and white. In general, meat pairs well with full-bodied reds like Cabernet Sauvignon or Zinfandel, and full-bodied whites like Viognier, but it's more important to just choose wines you particularly like. A few more wine tips to keep in mind:

• If you need to chill a bottle of white in a flash, stick the bottle in an ice bucket and fill the base with ice. Add a generous handful of salt—which makes the ice melt at a lower temperature—then more ice, layering until you reach the neck of the bottle. Fill the bucket with cold water. The wine should be ready to serve in about 10 minutes.

• One bottle of wine pours about four or five glasses, so for a party of eight, six bottles should be plenty.

• To pour wine like a pro, wrap a tea towel around the bottle to catch any drips (with chilled bottles, this also helps with insulation). Aim for the center of the glass, filling only about halfway to allow guests to swirl if they so choose, then twist the bottle slightly so that the last drip falls into the glass rather than down the side of the bottle (or your hands—classy!).

RUSTIC POTATO CENTERPIECES

Gather a few terra-cotta pots about six to eight inches high.

Wrap burlap around each pot, leaving extra material at the top so that you can tuck it down into the pot.

Tie a piece of raffia around the necks of the pots.

Fill with potatoes, placing the largest ones on the bottom and saving the prettiest ones (no blemishes!) for the top. Experiment with different varieties—red, Yukon gold, and russet.

Feel free to toss in herbs for added color, and use a few sprigs of dill or rosemary to fill in holes.

Henry Hashbrown

Happy Accidents

STICKY SITUATION: You start pouring the wine into guests' glasses—their WATER glasses.

HOSTESS RECOVERY: Make a joke of it and say, "Oops! I guess we'll be drinking wine like water today!" Then go ahead and pour water into the wineglasses. Sipping wine from casual water glasses actually perfectly matches the easy-breezy vibe you were going for. Drink to that!

STICKY SITUATION: Just before your guests are set to arrive, the sky opens up and it starts pouring rain. A couple of your guests were caught without an umbrella, and they run to your front door soaking wet!

HOSTESS RECOVERY: Get some towels and escort them to a bedroom or bathroom. Offer a blow-dryer, makeup, or anything else to help them get dry and put back together. When they reenter the party, tell them you appreciate them keeping in theme, as you always "fluff" your potatoes before you serve them, too! Your guests are now comfortable being a part of the party—dry and laughing!

OTHER SURPRISING CENTERPIECES BY SEASON

SPRING: Line the table with tea-cups filled with wheatgrass fresh out of the box.

SUMMER: Pack a long wooden crate with colorful vegetables like carrots, radishes, peppers, and broccoli florets.

FALL: Run mini white pumpkins down the length of the table.

WINTER: Fill Mason jars with white battery-powered twinkle lights.

TWISTS ON A THEME: MORE PARTY IDEAS FROM CHERYLSTYLE.COM

HOLA TO OLÉ: From the first hello (*hola*) to the excitement of new friends (*olé*), this festive meet-and-greet party keeps any fiesta from becoming a siesta. Feature a make-it-yourself taco bar and colorful fruit-infused margaritas to give your guests a chance to mingle, mariachi, and get to know each other.

COOKIES OLD-SCHOOL: Centered on parents of school-age children, this cookie exchange party adds nostalgia to the setting of meeting the other parents in your child's classroom and being reminded of all the lessons to learn in school for both your children and yourself. Warm cookies and milk are a sweet way to get to know each other.

Sophisticated Retro Baby Shower

*For marking the arrival of a new life
without the usual pastel trimmings...*

Throwing a baby shower doesn't have to mean pink-and-blue streamers, cutesy paper plates, and hours-long gift-opening sessions. But you do want the event to be special; after all, it's an incredibly magical thing to mark the arrival of a new life. This party puts a chic spin on the typical baby shower, with an unexpected retro palette of avocado green with slate blue and chocolate brown, decorations that double as take-home gifts for the mom-to-be, and a menu that celebrates the baby theme in a sophisticated way. It's so easy to put together, it's like taking candy from a . . . well, you know.

Little
Cutie

"For a hip mom-to-be, the standard pastel party just won't do—a retro theme feels more sophisticated. I fell for this polka-dot pattern because it made me think of the '60s."

"When I created this party for my friend Terry, I really wanted it to feel different than the same old showers we've all gone to in the past. So I zeroed in on one that would really scream 'Terry.' She's extremely down-to-earth and laid-back but has a chic streak in her—she loves fashion and mid-century design. I came up with the idea of throwing a retro-themed, back-to-basics shower that recalls the days when cloth diapers, traditional baby shoes, and glass baby bottles were the norm. Then I decided to serve baby-food-inspired dishes to up the fun factor. It's definitely not your everyday shower."

This party pairs classic baby elements with an elegant color scheme that keeps the look from feeling too kitschy. Glass baby bottles filled with freesia serve as centerpieces, a clothesline features onesies blowin' in the wind, and cloth diapers double as napkins; the mom-to-be can reuse all of these items. Even the place settings are retro baby-themed: easy-to-make vinyl bibs bring smiles (imagine looking around a table of bib-wearing adults).

HAVE FUN WITH THE MENU

Think "small." A first course of baby vegetable soup sets the infant mood, followed by delicious petit filet (get it?).

Dessert is sure to inspire oohs and aahs, with old-school baby shoes filled with vanilla ice cream drizzled with apricot puree (eaten with baby spoons, of course). Baby Bellinis—sparkling wine or apple cider mixed with apricot puree—allow even the mom-to-be to indulge in a round or two. You can also spruce up guests' water glasses with an ice cube surprise: fill ice cube trays halfway full, add raspberries, cherries, or sprigs of mint, then top off with water and freeze. To cut down on the amount of food you have to serve, and to allow guests to munch on something while you're bringing platters from the kitchen, set the table with low-carb fill-'er-up items like carrots and hummus, or tall glasses filled with crudités.

SHARE DISHWARE, TABLES & CHAIRS

Something my friends and I do for large gatherings is to borrow dishes from each other. I have a few pieces of beautiful iron compotes from an artist in Dallas. They're pricey, so over the years I'd treat myself to a piece now and then. When my friends saw them they fell in love too, and started collections of their own. Between the three of us, we now have about thirty pieces, so when we throw parties we borrow each other's. We all have different-style houses—modern, traditional, Spanish rustic—but something like iron works with everything. I often give my friends iron serveware that complements the compotes as gifts, too, so I never have to stress about what to give someone—I just add to the collection each year.

You can also contact a local party rental company to provide everything from glasses and silverware to ice buckets, chairs, and tables. (Here's a tip for when you're arranging multiple tables: Make sure to set them up with the chairs pulled out so there's enough room for people to walk through.) The best part of bringing in these items is that you can coordinate exactly when you want them, like a few hours before the party starts, say, and have them picked up that same night. I like the tables delivered the day before—so I can set up ahead of time and I'm free all the next day to focus on the food. Plus, most rental companies don't expect you to wash the dishes—you can just rinse and repack them. *Phew.*

SEND GUESTS HOME WITH A PRACTICAL PARTING GIFT

Hand out kits filled with mini bottles of hand sanitizer and other goodies for when they visit the baby. Consider personalizing the hand sanitizer at sites like beau-coup.com. This worked particularly well for Terry, since she's a self-proclaimed germaphobe, but it's ideal for everyone. It's more functional and original than the standard mints or decorated cookies.

Below: A toast for the mommy-to-be. Opposite, clockwise from top right: White fresia in glass baby bottles is a sweet—and fragrant—addition to the table; a new-baby survival kit makes the perfect gift; the almost too-cute-to-eat dessert—eating a baby-inspired dessert will bring out the kid in all of you.

ASK YOURSELF BEFORE YOU START

WHO'S COMING?
If it's a surprise, consider asking the guest of honor's mom or spouse for invitee suggestions. You'll want it to be intimate, so stick to close friends and family. Put it this way, if someone you're thinking of inviting doesn't know the guest of honor is pregnant, she probably shouldn't be invited.

WHEN SHOULD IT BE HELD?
Baby showers are typically held four to six weeks before the due date. Just make sure your guest of honor is OK with having a shower before the big day—some people are superstitious; others, religious.

WHO PAYS?
If you're throwing it, you're dishing out the dough. Consider sharing the duties and expenses with another close friend or family member.

CHILLING THE CHAMPAGNE

Forgot to put the bubbly in the fridge? The fastest way to chill Champagne is to plunge it in an ice bucket filled with half ice, half water. Thirty minutes should do it.

POPPING THE CORK

Still doing the point-and-shoot method? That way releases too much gas at once, and you end up losing a lot of precious bubbly. Instead, after taking off the wire surrounding the cork, hold the cork in one hand and with the other, slowly turn the bottle—not the cork—until it pops.

BABY BELLINIS

By creating two versions of these Baby Bellinis—one alcoholic, one nonalcoholic—all guests can indulge in a celebratory clink.

Ingredients:
Canned, fresh, or frozen peaches
Champagne or sparkling wine
Sparkling apple cider

Directions:
1. In a blender, mix peaches until they're smooth but still have some texture.
2. Spoon a tablespoon and a half of the mixture into each Champagne coupe.
3. You can set the coupes up on a table, with bottles of Champagne and sparkling apple cider nearby, and have guests pour the cocktail or mocktail to their liking, or you can pour Champagne into some glasses, apple cider into others, and label which is which.

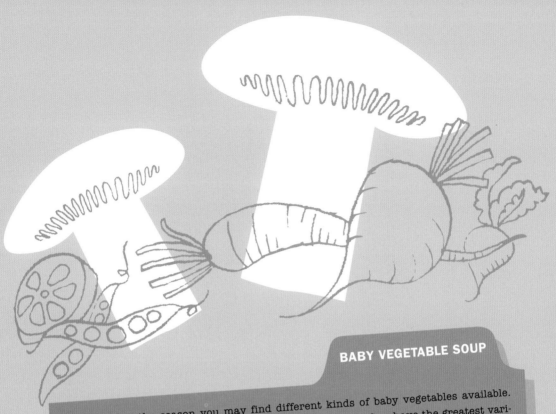

BABY VEGETABLE SOUP

Depending on the season you may find different kinds of baby vegetables available. Don't be afraid to mix and match. Farmers' markets will often have the greatest variety of baby delights. I also find that Asian markets often provide interesting options. I especially like enoki and beech mushrooms, which are becoming readily available in most markets. Their cute little size and rich flavor really add to the soup.

Serves 10 to 12
Prep time: 30 minutes
Total time: 1 hour 40 minutes
Ingredients:

4 cloves garlic
1 tablespoon chopped fresh flat-leaf parsley
1 tablespoon fresh thyme leaves
2 tablespoons grated ginger
2 tablespoons extra-virgin olive oil
2 large shallots, chopped
3 pounds mixed baby vegetables, halved (quartered if large)

1 tablespoon kosher salt
½ tablespoon ground white pepper
½ cup freshly squeezed lemon juice
12 cups chicken or vegetable stock
7 ounces beech mushrooms, stems cut off
7 ounces enoki mushrooms
Micro greens (optional)

Directions:

1. In a food processor, chop the garlic, parsley, thyme, and ginger to a fine paste. **2.** In a large pot, warm the oil over medium-low heat. Gently sauté the shallots until soft, about 4 minutes. Add the herb mixture and sauté for 2 minutes. **3.** Add the baby vegetables and cook until slightly tender, about 20 minutes. Add the salt, white pepper, and lemon juice and continue to cook for an additional 10 minutes, or until all the vegetables are starting to soften. **4.** Add the stock, cover, and bring to just under a boil. Reduce to a simmer for 40 minutes. **5.** Add the mushrooms and simmer for 5 minutes, then remove from the heat. **6.** Garnish with micro greens and serve warm.

This is one of those recipes that I say is "so easy even Cheryl could make it." It looks difficult to assemble, but it's super-easy and tastes delicious. Tucked into a baby shoe, it's almost too cute to eat—almost!

To prepare it, you'll need:

Vanilla ice cream
Small ice-cream scooper
Baking sheet
Canned apricots
Blender

Whole pistachios
Olive oil
Kosher salt
Small plastic cups to fit into shoes, chilled
Baby shoes (buy at any children's store)
Baby spoons

Directions:

1. Place scoops of ice cream on the baking sheet, a few inches apart. Slide the baking sheet into the freezer (freezing the scoops will keep them from melting as fast; you can do this the day before). **2.** To puree apricots: Pour into a blender; pulse to the consistency of baby food. **3.** To roast pistachios: On a baking sheet, chop with a knife to give them an organic shape. Spray with olive oil and a sprinkling of kosher salt. Place in a 375°F oven for about 10 minutes, or until brown. **4.** Right before serving, take ice cream out of the freezer, put a scoop in each cup, drizzle on the puree, then sprinkle with pistachios. Place the cup into a baby shoe, and serve (see photo, opposite).

·Serve onion dip or a bean salad in a carved-out red pepper.
·Use a hollowed-out pineapple to serve fruit salad.
·Place colorful food on bright white dishes, and white food on bold dishes—think hot pink or electric orange.
·Serve spinach dip in glass votives as individual appetizers
·Serve individual quiches in mini ramekins.

BABY-SHOWER BIBS

Creating baby-appropriate decor is kids' play with these simple steps.

Here's what you'll need to make 8 bibs:

* An old bib to trace around; if you don't have one, go to CherylStyle.com/book for a printable version.

* Safety pins

* Sharp scissors

* 8 yards of 1-inch thick rickrack trim

* Velcro

* Glue gun and glue sticks

* Puffy paint

* 2 yards of vinyl from a craft store

Work on a large surface covered with a drop cloth or newspaper.

1. Print out the bib pattern from CherylStyle.com/book, and cut it out. (If you have an old bib lying around, you can simply use that as a guide.) **2.** Secure the bib pattern (or actual bib) to the piece of vinyl with safety pins to keep it in place. Using the pattern as a guide, cut out the bib. **3.** Heat up your glue gun. Carefully glue rickrack trim around the edges of the bib, letting it hang about a quarter inch over the edges. Cut two 1-inch pieces of Velcro. **4.** Use the glue gun to attach the soft-sided Velcro to the "back" side of the upper-left-hand corner closure and the hooked side to the "front" of the other, making sure the position on one side matches up to the position on the other. Using puffy paint, carefully write each guest's name on a bib. Don't forget: The mother-to-be wears "Mommy."

DIAPER NAPKINS

For these retro diaper napkins, you'll need:

* Square cotton napkins or cloth
  diapers
* Diaper pins (or safety pins)

1. Lay your napkin on a flat surface. Fold it into a triangle with the point facing toward you. **2.** Fold the tip up so that it touches the top of the napkin. **3.** Fold both sides in toward the middle, using a diaper pin (or safety pin) to secure.

Party Highlights

NAME THAT BABY

Using letters from both the mom and dad's first names, guests have to create a name for the baby. Funniest gets a prize.

BABY GAMBLE

How about we make things interesting? On a side table, display a raffle box—anything from a birdcage to a cool vintage mailbox—and blank pieces of paper. Guests can write the date that they think the baby will be born, and toss in five bucks. Once the baby is born, the person who guessed correctly (or whoever's closest) gets to use that money to buy a group gift on behalf of everyone at the party.

MYSTERY BABY

Ask each guest to bring a photo of herself as a baby. Tape the photos to a bulletin board, with a number beneath each. Hand guests a sheet of paper with the partygoers' names listed. The first person to match the adult with their baby picture wins.

MEASURE THE MOM

Place a roll of twine and a pair of scissors on each table. Have each guest cut a piece of twine thought to be the distance around the mom-to-be's tummy. Whoever gets closest without going over wins.

GERBER GUESSING GAME

Buy fifteen or so jars of baby food in different flavors, take off the labels, and use a permanent marker to put a number on each lid. Place a few jars on each table, along with baby spoons, and have each guest sample the baby food and guess what the flavors are.

DRINKING CONTEST

Fill baby bottles—yes, complete with nipples—with apple juice, and see who can finish first. *Chug, chug, chug!*

WHAT'S IN THE BOX

Buy anywhere from ten to twelve baby items, such as a teething ring, a pacifier, and a bottle of baby powder. Put them in a box with a hole at the top only big enough for a hand to go inside. The guests have to feel around in the box and write down what they think is inside.

ONE-OF-A-KIND ONESIES

Indulge your guests' creative sides—and send mom home with a few "designer originals"—by setting up a station for decorating onesies. Buy a bunch of white onesies in various sizes, and tuck a piece of cardboard inside each to give it support. Prop the table with puffy paint and fabric markers. You can create one and put it on display to get things going—tell everyone to be as cute, silly, or sweet as they want.

Happy Accidents

STICKY SITUATION: You ask your daughter to help you with setting up the party. She misspells the guest of honor's name when printing out the menu cards, and there's not enough time to reprint them.

HOSTESS RECOVERY: Use them anyway—as is. During the toast, bring attention to the misspelling, and let the mom-to-be know that this is actually a peek into her future because once the baby is born, she won't remember her name anyway! You're sure to get a laugh, and this "mistake" is now part of the personality of the shower.

STICKY SITUATION: You're about to set the tables and realize you're two tablecloths short.

HOSTESS RECOVERY: Raid your linen closet for pretty bedsheets or blankets that you can alternate with the "real" tablecloths, and most likely you'll end up with a colorful, eclectic mix that has guests commenting on the cool factor.

TWISTS ON A THEME: MORE PARTY IDEAS FROM CHERYLSTYLE.COM

POO POO PARTY: Here's a party for friends who don't mind a little potty talk. It's your "doo-ty" to have fun at this yellow- and brown-themed party that features a potty chair full of daisies as a centerpiece and an invitation that comes tucked inside a disposable diaper. During those diaper-changing moments, memories of this party are sure to bring a chuckle.

BABY GENIUSES: For this baby-learning-themed party, ask guests to bring children's books and early childhood development toys with a personal inscription. Teach some baby sign language to the moms—it's a great way to nurture their brainpower and talk to their baby geniuses.

LABOR PARTY UNITE: Start this couples shower with a picket sign welcome for the expectant parents. Set the room like a union hall meeting, using divided trays as plates and tables named Local 123. The union boss (host/hostess) will collect union dues, which is a cash gift for the couple. This Labor Party is all about expectations!

Elegant Thanksgiving Potluck

*For hosting a relatively stress-free
(and Tupperware-free) holiday...*

"I came from a family that considered gravy a beverage." —Erma Bombeck

The mere thought of hosting Thanksgiving makes most people go out of their gourds. Here's something to be thankful for: You don't have to bite off more than you can chew. This year, take some pressure off and share the harvest while sharing key duties with friends and family. A "potluck plan" that you e-mail to guests will ensure that everyone takes on a dish and a role to help. (Uncle Bob is bringing the green beans—and taking out the trash.) You'll set up a beautiful buffet with as much attention to detail as you would a dinner table—with pretty platters at the ready for Aunt Edna to dole out her famous squash surprise.

"Everyone helps pull a potluck together, even kids—their art projects will double as decoration. I like bringing in a chalkboard to write down 'chores' so no one gets away with being a slacker!"

To-Do

"I came up with this potluck plan for Thanksgiving because, for years, my mom used to come over and cook everything. That's right. I'm a grown woman who would let her mom do all the cooking. But I recently decided that it just might be time to give my wonderful mom a break (although I didn't want to take it all on myself, either). Potlucks are so great because there's safety in numbers. You don't have to worry about being the star, the hero who miraculously pulled it together. By having guests contribute, the end result is often better than it would be if you did it all alone. You get to sample everyone else's handiwork, see how your best friend's grandmother perfects sweet potatoes, and learn that maybe you really do like deviled eggs after all. Many hands really do make light work, and there's just something about everyone sharing the duties that goes well with the generous, selfless feeling of Thanksgiving. There's a great quote that I often think of: 'It's amazing what you can get done when you don't care who gets the credit.' This way, you can focus more on being grateful—for your friends and family, and for all this delicious food (that you didn't have to make)."

CARVE THE WAY FOR A CAREFREE DAY

Before the gobble-down begins, assign guests tasks so everyone has a job to do and a dish to bring. One of the easiest ways is to create a Google document and e-mail it to your guests. They'll be able to volunteer for what they want and also see other people's responses—meaning no duplicates. One thing to remember: Tell whoever is bringing the turkey how many people you're expecting; a pound of turkey per person should be more than enough, with leftovers to spare. Day-of, write down duties on a chalkboard or sheet of paper that you display or even frame to remind everyone of their role. For a downloadable list of duties, visit CherylStyle.com/book.

BUFFET AWAY!

Creating a buffet frees up prime dinner-table real estate and allows you to create a gorgeous, abundant display. Have a variety of platters on hand—silver and white ceramic looks chic—so that guests can seamlessly transfer their dishes from Tupperware to table. Create different tiers—use cigar boxes or wooden risers—and place the turkey on the highest level so it's like all the other dishes are bowing down to its glory. To make sure you have enough room on the table, place the empty platters on the table the day before.

DESIGN A TASTEFUL TABLE

Unexpected elements make a table feel special. I like to serve gravy from a pretty metal flea-market-find coffeepot—the lid will keep the gravy hot, and the spout makes for a perfect pour with little mess. If you've got butterfingers in your family, use a brown tablecloth—it'll camouflage any gravy spills. For place settings, simple name cards tucked underneath chocolate-brown pen caps invite guests to write what they're thankful for on the flip side. Near the end of dinner, have one of the kids read aloud what was written and have guests try to guess the author.

CARVE OUT A COOL SPOT FOR KIDS

Everyone remembers being relegated to the wobbly kids' table, sitting with random cousins and sneaking pieces of turkey to the dog. Keep boredom at bay by covering the table with brown kraft paper; place crayons in empty soup cans (take off the labels) to inspire doodling. The best part of this "tablecloth" is the easy cleanup—you can toss it in the trash at day's end. Serve kids sparkling drinks: white grape juice with seltzer or simply seltzer with a lemon or lime dropped in a fancy glass. They'll feel super special.

Below: A table decorated with pumpkins and an overflowing cornucopia gives a sense of abundance. Opposite, from left: Use a chalkboard to delegate responsibilites and dishes among your guests; deck out the kids' table with kraft paper and crayons to keep little ones busy.

1. Make the tines shine · polish the silver   Sue
2. Put everyone in their place · set the table   Disa
3. Set the bar · pour drinks   Tim
4. Dish it up · plate food brought by guests   Mom
5. Make a wish · Debone the turkey   Bob
6. Say Abracadabra · Clear the table   Betty
7. _____ · Serve dessert   Piper
   _____ out the trash   Daddy
   _____ dishwasher   Cheryl
   _____ sher   Rebecca

A simple garnish can bring melancholy mashed potatoes or colorless creamed onions to life. Fill a deep tray with about an inch of water, and lay down fresh herbs like lavender, sage, thyme, parsley, rosemary, mint, cilantro, basil, lemon leaves, or kale leaves. For pops of color, think cranberries, pomegranate seeds, beets, radishes, and carrots. Place the tray on a side table with a cute sign that says something like "I'm here to dress up your dish." Urge guests to experiment, playing around with color, shape, texture, and taste. For instance, feathery, delicate dill balances the weight of cooked carrots, while shiny basil looks pretty on stuffing. Check out this handy chart to get your garnish juices flowing.

CHOOSE YOUR OWN GARNISH

	Herbs/Spices	Nuts/Seeds	Fruits	Unexpected Treats
Turkey	Lavender	Pomegranate seeds	Orange slices	Chunks of Parmesan
Yams/ Sweet potatoes	Sage	Cashews	Coconut shavings	Mini marshmallows
Cranberry sauce	Rosemary	Walnuts	Dried apricots	Crème fraîche
Green beans	Thyme	Toasted almonds	Mandarin oranges	Prosciutto
Cooked carrots	Dill	Baked pumpkin seeds	Dried cranberries	Brown sugar
Stuffing	Italian parsley	Pine nuts	Sliced green apple	Bacon strips
Peas	Rosemary	Pistachios	Diced tomatoes	Ham
Mashed potatoes	Chives	Pine nuts	Dried apple crisps	Sour cream dollop
Pumpkin pie	Cinnamon sticks	Sunflower seeds	Sour cherries	Pecan brittle

CRANBERRY CITRUS SAUCE

A tangy twist on a classic, this quick and easy homemade sauce is beautiful and delicious.

Serves 8
Prep time: 25 minutes
Total time: 1 hour

Ingredients:

1 small orange, unpeeled, sliced, seeds removed
2 cups orange juice
2 cups sugar
2 tablespoons freshly squeezed lemon juice

1 tablespoon freshly squeezed lime juice
2 (12-ounce) bags fresh cranberries
Orange zest, for garnish

Directions:

1. Finely grind the orange in a food processor. (Or finely chop the orange.) **2.** In a large saucepan, combine the orange juice, sugar, lemon juice, and lime juice. Bring to a boil, stirring until the sugar dissolves. Reduce the heat and simmer for 5 minutes. **3.** Add the ground orange and cranberries. Cook over medium heat until the berries begin to pop. Stir occasionally for about 8 minutes. The sauce will begin to thicken. Remove from the heat and let cool completely. **4.** Refrigerate. When ready to serve, garnish with orange zest. The sauce can be prepared up to 3 days ahead.

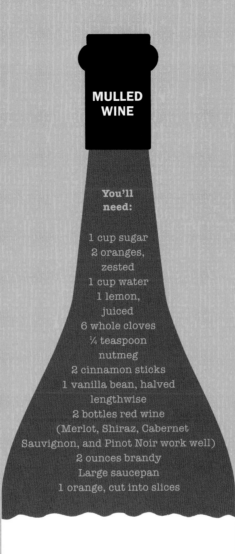

MULLED WINE

You'll need:

1 cup sugar
2 oranges, zested
1 cup water
1 lemon, juiced
6 whole cloves
¼ teaspoon nutmeg
2 cinnamon sticks
1 vanilla bean, halved lengthwise
2 bottles red wine (Merlot, Shiraz, Cabernet Sauvignon, and Pinot Noir work well)
2 ounces brandy
Large saucepan
1 orange, cut into slices

This warming drink sets a festive mood and makes your whole house smell amazing.

Directions:
1. Place sugar, zest, water, and lemon juice in a large saucepan. Add spices, vanilla, and about half a cup of wine. Bring to a boil for about 5 minutes; you want this to get thick and syrupy. **2.** Lower heat, add in the rest of the wine and the brandy until warm. **3.** Remove from heat and pour into a strainer to catch spices. **4.** Add orange slices, which will float on top. Ladle into cups.

STUFFED CORNUCOPIA

Start with a store-bought cornucopia or even a cone-shaped basket (to make the end pointier like a horn, steam it and pull to stretch it out). Bunch up some newspaper, straw, or raffia and place it in the back. Start with your largest fruits and veggies (artichokes, pomegranates), and then add smaller items like gourds, apples, ears of corn, and grapes so that your cornucopia runneth over. Lastly, sprinkle some nuts and berries on top to fill in any cracks.

BOWLING PIN TURKEYS

Even if you've never bowled a turkey (the term for three strikes in a row), at least you can make one. I got this idea from a wonderful friend of mine, Jen. It's a great project that will keep the little ones occupied and their creative juices flowing. Search for old bowling pins online, at thrift stores, or garage sales. Instruct kids to trace their hands onto construction paper and cut out the designs. These can be glued to the back of the pin for the tail feathers, and googly eyes used to create the face.

Party Highlights

A great way to make your potluck feel polished rather than thrown together is to decant the dishes your guests bring from those unsightly plastic containers into your own pretty serveware. It just changes the whole feel of the room. Before guests arrive, you can put Post-its on serving pieces so everyone knows which dish goes where (the mashed potatoes in the big white ceramic bowl, the string beans on the long thin silver platter). Best part? At the end of the day, everyone can use their containers to bring home any leftovers.

If you plan to freeze your leftovers, be sure to use containers designed specifically for the freezer. Label them clearly with the date and the name of the food, and organize your freezer so that the most recently frozen items move to the back.

KIDS CAN HELP TOO!

When planning any big family meal, don't forget that the kids can pitch in too! There are lots of ways kids can help with cooking, from mashing the potatoes and snapping string beans to tearing up herbs or cubes of bread for stuffing. If you make a particular dish each year, like a pumpkin pie from a recipe handed down through generations, kids can help make it and look forward to it each year. Children can also make great decorating "assistants"—have them fold napkins, put out the knives and forks, even create centerpieces, personalized place mats, or name cards for the table.

Happy Accidents

STICKY SITUATION: Aunt Judy signs up to bring her leaves-much-to-be-desired fruitcake.

HOSTESS RECOVERY: Give her a call and say, "Thank you so much for the offer, but we have lots of cakes on the menu already. I'd love you to bring a bottle of Champagne and give a toast." Crisis averted—she's happy to have a special role at dinner, and no one has to choke down fruitcake with a smile.

STICKY SITUATION: The person who signed up for the appetizer is late, and your guests have started to arrive.

HOSTESS RECOVERY: Grab that green salad you made, dole out small portions into juice glasses, throw a cracker on top of each, and place on a side table alongside some forks. Taking away the large salad bowl you had on the buffet now frees up a spot for people to put plates down as they dish out their meal, so it worked out better anyway!

TWISTS ON A THEME: MORE PARTY IDEAS FROM CHERYLSTYLE.COM

BLACK FRIDAY BRUNCH: Gather your girlfriends at the crack of dawn to shop the sales, and then come back home to share the spoils of the day. This is best done over a custom-made Bloody Mary, followed by a delicious post–Turkey Day brunch where everyone's thankful to have gotten a start on their holiday shopping.

TURKEY, TAKE 2: Create the usual fixings in fun finger-food form: turkey sliders, stuffing, mashed potatoes, sweet potatoes, squash soup, and peas all served in small cocktail glasses. Serve bite-sized pumpkin pies from large tasting spoons.

GET YOUR GOBBLE ON!: Set up a turkey chili bar; a mashed potato bar with chives, cheese and sour cream; and a pumpkin pie bar with sweet toppings: crème fraîche, ricotta cheese, pecan brittle and maple syrup. And while everyone's getting stuffed, conduct a neighborhood food drive to help others get their gobble on, too.

Swashbuckling Walk-the-Plank Pirate Party

For that naughty—but lovable!—little boy in your life
(and his scalawag friends)...

"There's a good time coming, boys! A good time coming."
—Charles MacKay

Ahoy, mateys! It's time to host a swashbuckling birthday party for yer little lad. If it's something special ye be after, this here's the ticket: a great, grand day filled with buried treasure, booty galore, hearty grub (and grog), and high-sea adventures that yer hearties be talkin' 'bout for years to come. They'll forget all about thee real-life woes and venture on into the land of fantasy and fun. Walking the plank is just one of the surprising happenings that will befall yer lads. With "real" pirate goods—sand, coins, mustaches, hats, you name it—they will get right in the seafaring spirit. Don't forget to invite a few landlubbers (they just might be bringin' some gold doubloons, shiver me timbers!). Arrr, gentleman of fortune, forge ahead!

"Pirate-motif paper plates and cups? Nah. I want kids to feel like they're really sailing the high seas. A table topped with sand, gold coins, and bandanna napkins will get them in the mood."

"If you really want to impress a little boy, truly let him be a little kid for a day. This party indulges his boys-will-be-boys side—at least for today. I threw this party for my friend's son Jack, who tends to get into a pickle now and then, if you know what I mean. He'll sneak potato chips from the cupboard two minutes before dinner, or bounce his basketball in the house when his mom is in another room. So I knew a party where he's actually allowed to be "naughty" was perfect for him. Here, he could wear tattoos and mustaches with his friends, chow on some turkey legs, and walk the plank—literally."

BUCKLE UP THE KIDS

As the little ones arrive, hand out eye patches, clip-on gold hoop earrings, big belts, and red bandannas—if you can find some with skulls on them, even better. Walk around with a black eyeliner to give kids crazy curly mustaches, and give kids temporary tattoos on their arms to add to the bravado.

BUST OUT A BOOTYLICIOUS TABLE

Use a rustic wood table if you can—it'll look like the base of a pirate ship—and place a wooden plank down the middle, the long way. Mix brown rice with raw sugar and pour it into mounds on either end to look like sand, and scatter plastic gems, bones, and skulls— you can finds these at party supply stores— along with gold coins in the "sand." Write "fish bait" on a silver pail with permanent marker or paint and fill with gummy worms and other slithery creatures. For place settings, use black bandannas as "place mats," topped with canvas napkins that you draw on (think dashes and palm trees and spiders) to look like an X-marks-the-spot treasure map. A plastic sword is the utensil, which the little pirates can use to spear pieces of fruit (sword kebabs, anyone?). On the back of each chair, hang a drawstring bag labeled with each kid's name and filled with loot like plastic necklaces.

YO HO HO AND A BOTTLE OF H$_2$O

I'm not into serving kids soda or even juice—I'd rather give 'em some healthy pirate grog—in this case, good old-fashioned water. But you can customize the labels on these mini bottles by going to CherylStyle.com/book. We put a white skull and crossbones on a black background and wrote "Poison" but you could also write "Jack's Brew."

GNAW ON YER PIRATE GRUB

When pirates eat, they do it in excess, so bake up some big turkey legs that are even bigger than some of yer kids' heads. Fish-stick "pirate fingers" recall what pirates would eat when they'd land in port and also play into the boys' gruesome sides (trust me, they'll love them). A watermelon ship, filled with fruit and complete with a *Jolly Roger* flag, is a great way to prevent scurvy. But of course, all little swashbucklers need something sweet: Skull sugar cookies are sure to satisfy their lily-livers!

Creative touches like skull-and-crossbones water bottles and a watermelon pirate ship make this table irresistibly naughty.

Serves 10
Total Time: 4-½ hours
Prep time: 30 minutes

TASTY TURKEY LEGS

You'll need:
10 turkey legs, trimmed
3 cups barbecue sauce
Cooking spray

Directions:
1. Preheat oven to 350°F. **2.** Pat legs dry. **3.** Brush legs liberally with your favorite barbecue sauce (or use sauce below). Place legs in a deep pan and roast for 2–2½ hours or until internal temperature is 180 degrees. Spray with cooking oil after 1 hour to prevent dryness. **4.** Take out and allow to cool for 15 minutes.

Barbecue Sauce

Ingredients:

2 cups ketchup
¼ cup apple cider vinegar
1½ cups honey
⅛ tablespoon freshly ground black pepper
½ tablespoon onion powder
½ tablespoon dry mustard
1 tablespoon freshly squeezed lemon juice
1 tablespoon Worcestershire sauce

Directions:
In a medium saucepan, combine all the ingredients with 1 cup water and bring to a boil. Reduce the heat to a simmer. Cook, uncovered, for 1½ hours, stirring occasionally. The sauce can be made a day in advance and kept in the refrigerator, tightly covered.

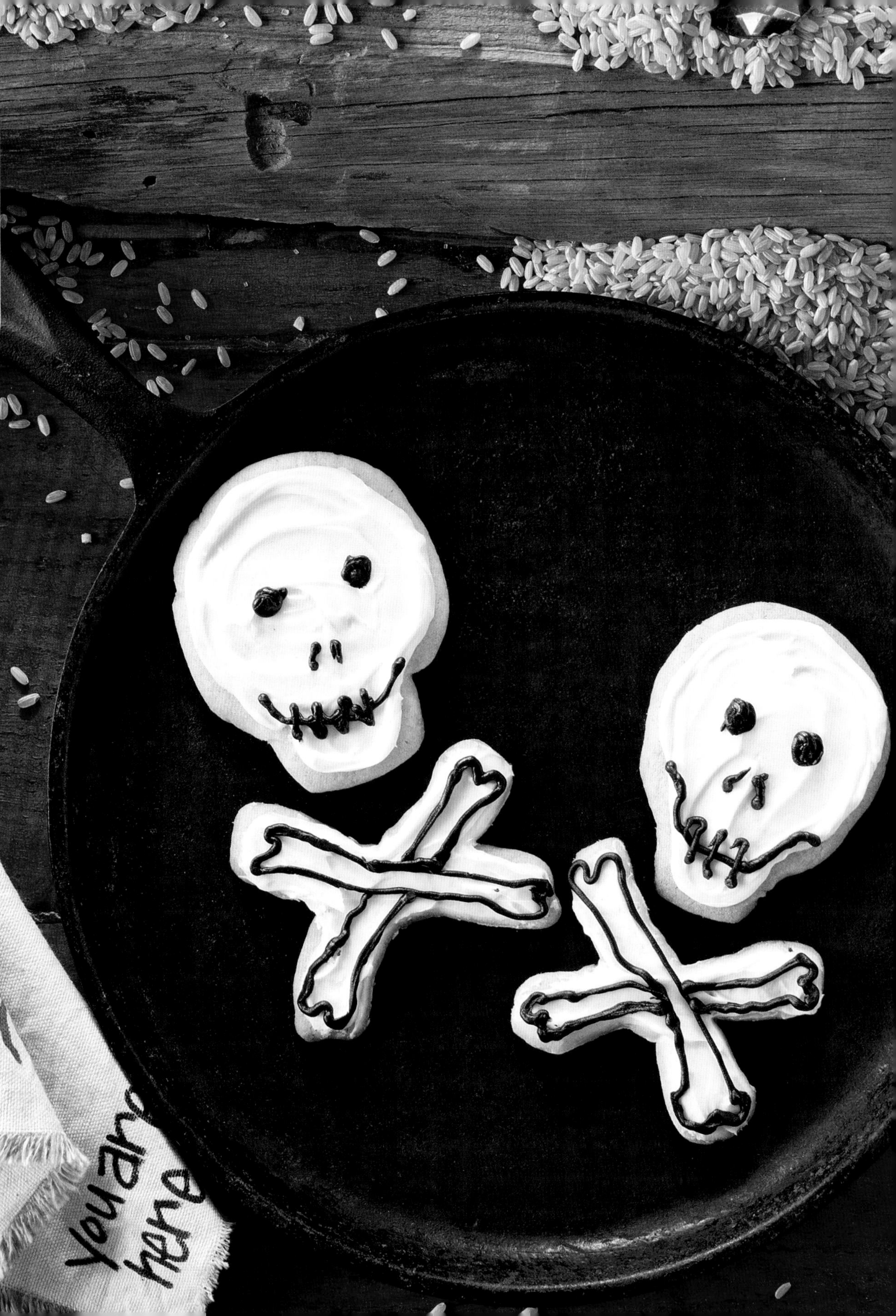

SKULL SUGAR COOKIES

You don't have to make your own icing of course, but if you want to go all out, be my guest.

Makes 36
Prep time: 1 hour 30 minutes
Total time: 2 hours 30 minutes

Cookie Ingredients:
2½ cups all-purpose flour
1 teaspoon baking soda
½ teaspoon baking powder
1 cup (2 sticks) unsalted butter, softened
1¼ cups sugar
1 large egg
½ teaspoon pure vanilla extract

Icing Ingredients:
6 cups confectioners' sugar
1 cup vegetable shortening
⅓–½ cup milk
1 teaspoon pure vanilla extract
Dash of kosher salt
Black food coloring or black icing

Cookie Directions:

1. Preheat the oven to 375°F. **2.** In a medium bowl, combine the flour, baking soda, and baking powder. **3.** In a large bowl, cream together the butter and sugar until smooth. Beat in the egg and vanilla. Gradually stir in the dry ingredients 1 cup at a time. Gather into a large ball, wrap in plastic wrap, and chill for 2 hours or overnight. **4.** Cut the ball into 4 portions. Three of these portions will be used for the skull shapes. The fourth will be for the crossbones. Work in batches as you bake, leaving the unrolled dough in the refrigerator so that the dough is cool as it enters the oven. **5.** Roll out one portion of dough on a lightly floured surface to about ¼ inch thickness. Cut 3-inch circles and remove excess dough; gather the extra dough into a ball and return it to the refrigerator. Using a sharp knife, cut the jawline of the skeleton head, starting about one-third of the way from the top of the circle and creating a diagonal line. When you are about one-third of the way into the cookie, change direction and cut directly down. Repeat on the other side of each circle and arrange on a baking sheet. Bake for about 8 minutes, until golden. Let stand on the baking sheet for 2 minutes before removing to wire racks to cool. **6.** For crossbones, cut 36 (2-by-1-inch) rectangles and with a knife create a long "X" by cutting triangles out of each side of each rectangle. Arrange on baking sheet, bake, and cool as above.

Icing Directions:

1. In a large bowl, using an electric mixer, cream together the confectioners' sugar and shortening until smooth. Gradually beat in the milk, vanilla, and salt. Remove ½ cup of the icing to a small bowl and add black food coloring to make a rich black color. **2.** When the cookies are completely cool, cover all of them with white icing. Allow them to set for 1 hour, uncovered. **3.** Fit a pastry bag with a round No. 2 or 3 piping tip and fill it with the black icing; use it to outline the shape of the skull and crossbones.

WATERMELON PIRATE SHIP

To Make the Sail:

1. Buy a few wooden dowels—we used one long one and two shorter ones to create the mast. **2.** Cover with black spray paint; let dry. **3.** Tie together with cooking twine to create a double T. **4.** Dip a length of cheesecloth into Stiffy Fabric Stiffener (available at craft stores). Tie to top and bottom short dowels while still wet. Mold the cheesecloth over a sink to design the "windblown" look of your sails. Let dry overnight.

To Make the Ship:

1. Look at the watermelon to see which side seems the flattest. Using a long sharp knife, slice a piece of rind off that side to stabilize the boat. Don't cut too deep—you don't want the boat to leak and capsize. **2.** With a permanent marker, draw the outline of a ship in a staircase design. Do this on both sides. **3.** Work in sections. Take your knife and carefully carve along the drawn line, taking off the top when you can and continuing until you have completed design. **4.** Using a large spoon, carve out the melon and set aside. **5.** Place sail (see above) into the fruit boat and press into the base. **6.** Cut up a variety of mixed fruit (including the watermelon you just removed) and place in boat.

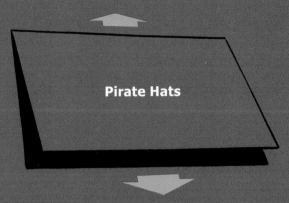

Pirate Hats

1. Fold a sheet of 11-by-17-inch black construction paper in half toward you (the flap should be facing you).

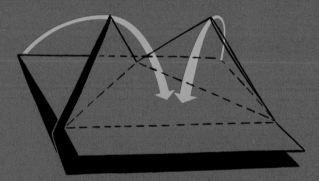

2. Fold each top corner toward the center to create two triangles. Fold up a flap (just one sheet), then flip the hat over and do the same for the other side. Use double-stick tape to secure the edges.

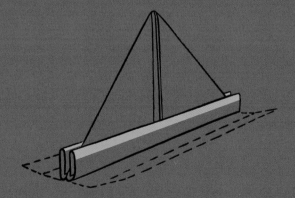

3. Glue a piece of gold ribbon on the edges to add some bling.

Party Highlights

COUPON BOOK

I always like to give a surprise at the end of the party, just when the guest of honor thinks all the surprises are over. This coupon book is a terrific idea, especially for a boy who tends to get into trouble.

Coupons can include:

* Good for riding your scooter in the house for ten minutes.

* Good for letting the hose run in the yard and playing in the mud.

* Good for not taking a shower for three days.

* Good for jumping on the bed for five minutes straight.

Have fun with it, and really cater the coupons to what you know your boy would love to do. It's easy and a surefire hit—and it's free!

WALK THE PLANK!

Set a wooden plank about a foot wide on the ground—you can also put it across a shallow fountain if you have one. Blindfold kids with bandannas and have them walk the plank. Whoever gets across without toppling gets some booty.

SCAVENGER HUNT

You can create your own, but for a much easier and less time-consuming way, consider buying a ready-made scavenger game that does all the work for you. InCLUEsive (incluesivecreations.com) is a game that lets kids decipher clues (in the form of brain teasers and riddles) to get to the next hiding place.

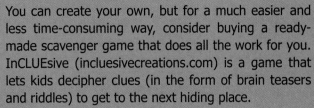

Happy Accidents

STICKY SITUATION: The party game used a real plank, and the first kid on it broke it!

HOSTESS RECOVERY: Shout out: "All hands on deck!" Make a new "plank" by having a couple of the boys get out the duct tape, and tape a "plank" onto the patio floor. Change the game to add "circling sharks"; the contestant has to be blindfolded and walk the plank without hitting the "sharks." The outcome is that more kids were involved in the game at the same time, and for the boys it was more fun to be the sharks anyway!

TWISTS ON A THEME: MORE PARTY IDEAS FROM CHERYLSTYLE.COM

GREAT BALLS OF FIRE: Trade swords for balls of all kinds! This bouncing party features an organized game of kickball and all manner of other ball games. The invite comes on a paddle-ball, and the kids will munch on melon balls, meatballs, popcorn balls, and cake pops. Use mitts as place mats to catch all the fun!

BIKER TYKES ON TRIKES: Let your boys go hawg-wild for this party, where they bring their own trike for an obstacle-course race. After decking out a leather vest and spiking their hair, the boys can trick out their trikes and try to become "king of the road"!

Holiday Coffee Drop-In

*For carving out time with friends
during this buzzing, bustling season...*

Sure, it's supposed to be the most wonderful time of the year. But is it, really, when you're trying to pack in shopping, wrapping, decorating, and some-how finding time to see family and friends without losing your mind? Sounds like the most stressful time of year to me. This season, carve out a two-hour time period one morning where you can see every one of your friends at once while drinking yummy flavored coffee and sampling a few bite-sized snacks. (And no, it's not a faux pas to put a start and end time on the invite.) Make it an open house so people can come and go as they please, so there's constant turnover and conversation stays lively. And turn decorating the house into a fun, inspiring experience rather than a chore by jazzing up your usual color palette with some eye-catching extras. Now, *that's* joy to the world.

"An offbeat holiday color scheme makes for instant festivity. I went for pops of orange to break up the sea of red and green, and black-and-white checkered ribbons as a fun twist on traditional tartan plaid."

"This is such a no-fail, no-stress party, and I know that because I've been hosting it for fifteen years! (My friend Robin has come to every single one, so she can vouch for me.) It all started one year when I realized that with the craziness of the holidays, I hadn't made any plans to see some of the people who mean the most to me—my girlfriends. I was too overwhelmed with other engagements to plan an all-out cocktail party, but the holidays just seemed amiss without the girls. So I thought, What do we all need to keep us going through this busy season? Coffee! It's an easy-to-make crowd-pleaser, and casual enough so that people feel they can drop in and out without pressure."

TIS THE SEASON . . .

Decorating in red and green? Been there, done that! Try decking the halls differently. I like to throw a curveball but still keep it festive. Go for bright red with chartreuse instead, and add shots of orange. For the tree, forgo traditional tinsel or garland for a bold orange boa—it's like playing dress-up for your tree. This is also a great time to pull out your sentimental silver. Around the house, especially on the mantel and buffet tables, be generous with twinkly metallic accents like silver candleholders, platters, and coffee urns; they bounce light around the room and make the whole room feel special.

PERK UP THE TABLE

Gift-wrapped boxes on a buffet table are a fun and festive departure from floral centerpieces. They create tiers which you can put food on, too. Try to wrap your boxes in an unexpected way that makes guests stop and notice. I like to keep the wrapping paper itself consistent—in this case, red—and then make each ribbon treatment a little different. One red box may have an orange ribbon, one may have a black-and-white striped ribbon, so that they share the same palette but each has a distinct personality. (Make certain to keep bows on one end of the packages if you're going to stack them.) Keep in mind that you can use this gift-wrap centerpiece idea for all kinds of parties—graduations, birthdays, wedding showers, you name it. Crystal goblets filled with green, orange, and red M&M's pull together the palette and invite nibbling. (I'm a sucker for M&M's.)

SAY ALL YOU WANT FOR CHRISTMAS IS . . . NOTHING

If guests ask what they should bring, tell them a gift for a child, which you can donate to a charity after the party. Sometimes in all the hustle and bustle we lose track of what the season is truly about.

Below: Gift-wrapped boxes create visually interesting tiers on a table. Opposite, clockwise from top right: decadent cheesecake pops are easy to eat while chatting; at a party where you need to keep mingling, a tray in hand is your best friend; frothy, festive coffee is a crowd-pleaser.

GIVE THE GIFT OF CAFFEINE

Serve various kinds of coffee in pretty urns so that guests can help themselves. Write each kind of coffee on a small card and place it in a small bowl filled with coffee beans in front of each urn. Include napkins, spoons, cream, and sugar on each end of the table to make it easier for guests to keep the flow moving.

HOW TO WORK THE ROOM

ZOOM IN AND OUT

To avoid getting held up in a long conversation, always hold a tray of food. That way, you can dip into a pocket of conversation, say a few words, dole out nibbles, and duck away to the next group. Another smart trick is to position your buffet table far from the table with the coffee urns. This keeps guests moving from station to station. Also know that guests often follow the host back into the kitchen, causing a traffic jam. So the less you go in there, the better.

BRING OUT THE BITE-SIZED SNACKS

Quick and easy no-mess finger foods allow you and your guests to indulge while standing and socializing. Plus, no utensils results in easier cleanup for you. Some of my favorites for brunch time include egg salad in endive, small roasted tomato quiches, mini pieces of banana bread, and, for dessert, cake pops and cheesecake squares. So decadent!

Fabulous Flavored Coffee

You can have so much fun experimenting with different brews. Here are a few of my all-time favorites for the holidays. These ideas are for a pot of coffee, but you can adapt them for coffee urns; just keep in mind how many cups your urn brews (most are 25, 40, or 55 cups) and experiment until you find what tastes right to you.

Eggnog Coffee

Add a cup of eggnog (store-bought is fine) to a pot of black coffee, followed by a few teaspoons of vanilla extract. Put out a bowl of whipped cream for dollops, and a shaker filled with nutmeg for a garnish.

Mexican Coffee

You'll add cocoa powder and cinnamon directly into the coffee grounds. Figure about a scoop of cocoa powder and half a teaspoon of cinnamon per four scoops of coffee, plus a dash of nutmeg. Garnish with whipped cream and cinnamon.

Peppermint Coffee

Add a cup of chocolate syrup (yes, you can use Hershey's) and half a cup of peppermint syrup to a pot of coffee. Use whipped cream to garnish.

Toffee Coffee

To a pot of coffee, add a cup of cream and a cup of brown sugar.

Spiced Coconut Coffee

Add a teaspoon crushed red pepper (yes, you read that right), four whole cloves, and a cinnamon stick to coffee grounds. Let the coffee brew. Meanwhile, heat a cup of coconut milk and a quarter cup of honey on the stove, stirring until the honey fully melts. Pour coffee into the mixture; this makes two mugs.

Not a coffeemaker?

You can hire a coffee caterer to save you the hassle of making the brew (and cleaning the urns). Or buy prebrewed coffee from Starbucks or Dunkin' Donuts and pour it into your urn so it looks like you made it yourself. (I won't tell.) Raid the bakery for cookies and other goodies and display them on a platter. Faced with a big pile of delicious-looking cookies, I really don't think guests will care if you made them or not. Do you?

Makes about 30; serves 10
Prep time: 30 minutes
Total time: 45 minutes

Ingredients:

12 large eggs
1 medium red onion, chopped
1 rib celery (with leaves), chopped
½ cup mayonnaise
2 tablespoons chopped fresh dill, plus more for garnish
2 tablespoons whole-grain mustard
2 tablespoons freshly squeezed lemon juice
¼ teaspoon kosher salt
½ teaspoon freshly ground black pepper
6 heads Belgian endive
Paprika

Directions:

1. Put the eggs in a large saucepan with cold water to cover by 2 inches. Bring to a boil and cook for 1 minute. Remove from the heat, cover, and set aside for 12 minutes. Drain and rinse the eggs in cold running water. Peel the eggs and chop them. **2.** In a large bowl, combine the onion, celery, mayonnaise, dill, mustard, lemon juice, salt, and pepper. Gently fold in the eggs and set aside. **3.** Cut the base off each head of endive and separate the leaves. Arrange on a baking sheet or serving platter. With a tablespoon, scoop the egg salad onto the endive leaves and garnish with paprika and fresh dill. Serve immediately.

20 NO-COOK APPETIZERS

1. Tomato and mozzarella skewers
2. Blue cheese crackers drizzled with honey
3. Fresh ricotta paired with walnut bread
4. Turkey breast, red pepper strips, and provolone rolled up in Bibb lettuce
5. Cucumber slices topped with cottage cheese
6. Pesto (from a jar) smeared on slices of Italian bread
7. Tortilla wraps filled with sun-dried tomatoes, arugula, and cream cheese
8. Bagel chips topped with lox spread
9. Individual tortilla chips topped with salsa and shredded cheddar
10. Mini goat cheese balls (roll with chopped hazelnuts or pistachios)
11. Olives and feta served on flatbread crackers
12. Figs stuffed with cream cheese and almonds
13. Dried apricots topped with blue cheese
14. Prosciutto-wrapped pear slices
15. Crostini with crab salad
16. Flatbread with roast beef and avocado slices
17. Roasted red pepper and basil skewers
18. Ritz crackers topped with pepperoni slices
19. Avocado-stuffed plum tomatoes
20. Baguette slices topped with onion paste

STORE-BOUGHT DESSERT SPRUCE-UP FOR ANY TIME OF YEAR

It's easy to turn supermarket finds into decadent treats—your guests will think you slaved away all day.

Bite-sized chocolate chip cookies: Use vanilla ice cream to make pop-in-your-mouth ice cream sandwiches. Freeze, then take them straight out of the freezer before you serve.

Brownie mix: Using small ramekins, bake brownies until they're just underdone. Top with mint chip ice cream for an ooey-gooey dessert you have to spoon out of the pan!

Pound cake: Slice into strips, stack into a fun pile, then serve warm chocolate sauce in small shot glasses so guests can pour it over the cake themselves.

Vanilla cake: Cut into small squares, then layer with vanilla pudding, whipped cream, and almonds in a wineglass for an easy parfait.

Bite-sized sugar cookies: Spread with Nutella and sprinkle with chopped pecans.

Vanilla ice cream: Sprinkle crushed toffee and hot fudge on top and serve in teacups.

Bananas: Place a candy-apple stick in each lengthwise and freeze; cover with melted chocolate and freeze again.

Angel food cake: Cut into 4-by-4-inch squares. Top with dollops of whipped cream and sprinkle with crushed raspberries.

Chocolate pudding: Layer pudding in a tall, sleek Tom Collins–style glass with sliced bananas and almonds. Top with a dollop of peanut butter you've mixed with agave syrup— the syrup will thin the peanut butter just enough to make it more like the consistency of pudding for a nice texture match.

Chocolate-covered matzo: I always love peanut butter sandwiches for dessert. You can find chocolate-covered matzo at Passover time. Break the matzo into pieces and cover with peanut butter and chocolate shavings. Graham crackers are great here too.

Marshmallows: Dip in melted chocolate and let cool. Thread onto a skewer with bananas and strawberries for a kid-friendly kebab-style dessert.

Spice cake: Cut into bite-sized pieces. Add a smear of mascarpone or cream cheese on top, insert a toothpick, and you have a sweet-and-spicy taste sensation.

Small croissants: Heat in the oven; when they're piping hot, drizzle warm caramel sauce on top and garnish with toasted almonds or mini chocolate chips. This ooey-gooey treat is great for dessert or brunch.

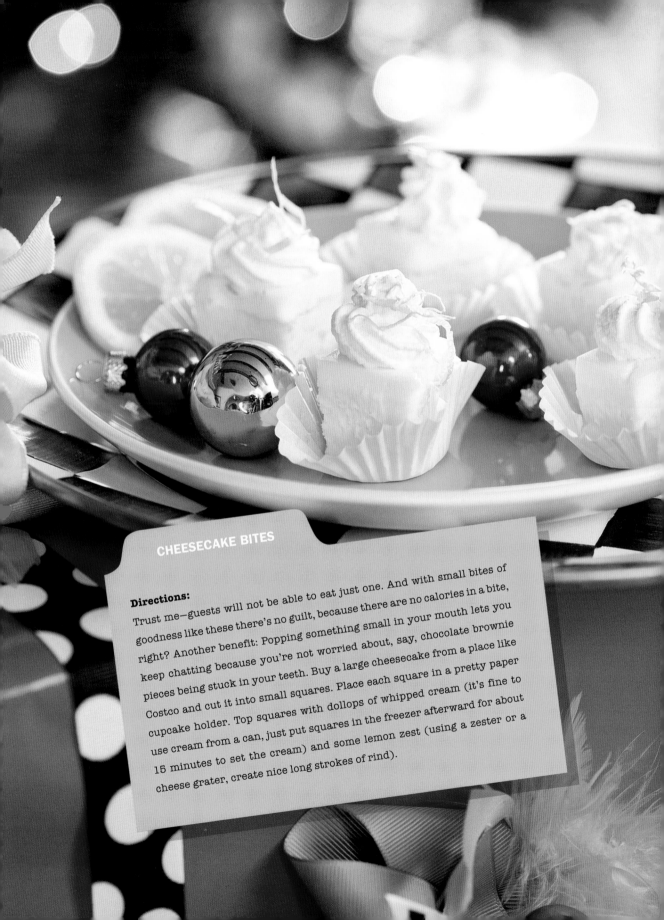

CHEESECAKE BITES

Directions:

Trust me—guests will not be able to eat just one. And with small bites of goodness like these there's no guilt, because there are no calories in a bite, right? Another benefit: Popping something small in your mouth lets you keep chatting because you're not worried about, say, chocolate brownie pieces being stuck in your teeth. Buy a large cheesecake from a place like Costco and cut it into small squares. Place each square in a pretty paper cupcake holder. Top squares with dollops of whipped cream (it's fine to use cream from a can, just put squares in the freezer afterward for about 15 minutes to set the cream) and some lemon zest (using a zester or a cheese grater, create nice long strokes of rind).

DRESS UP A PRESENT

I love giving gifts more than I enjoy receiving them. When I give a gift, I like it to be special, almost as if the wrapping is part of the gift itself, and then the actual gift is just a bonus. It shows that you literally took time out of your day to focus on this gift and make it special. When I wrap gifts I take care to use two different kinds of ribbon—one as the main, and another as an accent. And I almost always include a piece of boa tucked under the ribbon. Keep a few boas where you store your gift wrap; snip two-inch pieces off and tuck them inside the ribbon knot for some flair.

15 WAYS TO PUMP UP YOUR PARTY WITH COLOR

From decorating my tree to wrapping my gifts, I'm addicted to color. These ideas will brighten your table or room—and the mood of your gathering.

1. Float red or purple rose petals in a shallow bowl of water.

2. Top the dining table with a turquoise, green, or hot-pink runner—or try tying several silk scarves together.

3. Spread bright cocktail napkins out in a pinwheel shape.

4. Wrap a vase with colorful fabric before you put in your flowers.

5. Tie chair backs with bright ribbon.

6. Cut bold blooms like Gerber daisies low and display in squat containers.

7. Top white serving dishes with vivid foods like asparagus, beets, or strawberries.

8. Serve vibrant cocktails when guests arrive. Think green-apple martinis or Blue Lagoons (vodka, blue curaçao, and lemonade).

9. Replace standard lightbulbs for red, blue, green, or purple ones for oomph (check out 1000bulbs.com).

10. Toss a striped throw across the table for a splash.

11. Fill glass vases with gum balls. Put pink in one, blue in another, and so on.

12. Use craft fabric as place mats or napkins.

13. Cluster plants together for a surge of green.

14. Frame children's masterpieces as place mats to inject a sense of fun and playfulness.

15. Secure a piece of thick grosgrain ribbon to the bottom of a candlestick or vase.

Happy Accidents

STICKY SITUATION: You decided to hire a coffee caterer, and uh-oh . . . a no-show.

HOSTESS RECOVERY: Pull out the French press, the two Mr. Coffees in the cupboard, that percolator your mom gave you, and some thermoses. Ask your first arriving guests to help you, the hostess, in your "coffee klutch." Guests often want to know they were a help to the hostess, and guests that used to be mere acquaintances now work together for you and become friends. One of the proven ways to make a friend is to ask for a small measure of help—or a Starbucks run.

TWISTS ON A THEME: MORE PARTY IDEAS FROM CHERYLSTYLE.COM

HOLIDAY EFFERVESCENCE: This party sparkles with a few fun, festive punches in pretty bowls. The beauty of this, like Holiday Coffee, is that you make it and forget it—guests will help themselves so you're free to navigate the party. Go for a mix of flavors and colors. You can make a frothy pineapple-orange punch with scoops of lemon and lime sherbet floating on top, a lighter cranberry-citrus punch, and a sparkling Champagne and strawberry concoction.

HAUTE CHOCOLATE HOLIDAY: A high-fashion tree dressed to impress starts a party that will be sa-weet. Think boas, pearls, and gloves. Serve all different kinds of hot cocoa—white hot chocolate, mint hot chocolate, and various toppings, plus decadent chocolate martinis. Add a formal chocolate tasting to make this party really haute. If this doesn't sate the sweet tooths in your life, I don't know what will.

Resource Guide

Need your own party ideas? There are so many online ways to get inspired, which led me to design my own CherylStyle StyleBoard! This is the fastest and most fun way to imagine your party. Go to CherylStyle.com and Create a Moment! I'll type in something—say, "pirate party"—and see what pictures and other words come up. This helps me "name" my party, and I go from there! I also use Google Images and Pinterest.com for images, but only my StyleBoard brings the words and images together for my purpose. Here are some other sites to help turn your imagined party into a reality:

GENERAL PARTY SUPPLIES

Orientaltrading.com:
Amazing prices on themed goods, whether you're hosting a luau or an Oscar bash.

Etsy.com:
Here's how to really make your party feel unique. Handmade items, from polka-dot cupcake liners to pom-pom'd party hats are anything but run-of-the-mill.

Beau-coup.com:
The place for favors of all flavors! Think personalized lip balm and customizable playing cards.

INVITATIONS

Cardstore.com:
This site features a great selection of printable invites, from birthday parties to dinner parties.

Hallmark.com:
I love browsing this classic site for inspiration.

Foryourparty.com:
A fabulous place for design-your-own coasters, matchboxes, and napkins.

Minted.com:
Modern and fresh invite designs, with ultra-cute images.

DECOR

Save-on-crafts.com:
A great source for birch and manzanita branches (they make great table runners!), twinkle lights, and battery-powered candles.

Oliveandcocoa.com:
Go to the "Floral" section for beautiful flower arrangements in unexpected vessels like bark and wooden troughs.

Mjtrim.com:
You're sure to find "all the trimmings" here; there's an unbelievable selection of fabric, ribbons, appliqués, sequins, and more.

Pearlriver.com:
The best spot to find colorful paper lanterns, paper garlands, and pretty nylon parasols.

Shopsweetlulu.com:
Sweet striped straws, houndstooth treat bags, and hot-pink and lavender polka-dot birthday candles that would make a little girl shriek with joy.

TABLETOP

Westelm.com:
The place mats and napkins here look so much more expensive than they are.

CB2.com:
Check the "party stuff" section for ultra-modern yet affordable pitchers, ice buckets, and trays.

Surlatable.com:
Beautiful, well-priced serveware, from gravy boats to cake stands. Also check it out for outdoor pieces—they have adorable paper ice cream bowls.

Napastyle.com:
You'll find everyything from mod-looking glass decanters to pewter pitchers that look like they've been in the family for generations.

Williams-Sonoma.com:
Gorgeous ceramic serving pieces, and nice pewter and wooden chargers, too.

Index

Credits and Acknowledgments

CherylStyle

www.CherylStyle.com

This book was produced by

MELCHER MEDIA

124 West 13th Street
New York, NY 10011
www.melcher.com

President and Publisher: Charles Melcher
Associate Publisher: Bonnie Eldon
Editor in Chief: Duncan Bock
Senior Editor: Holly Dolce
Editor: Megan Worman
Production Director: Kurt Andrews
Production Coordinator: Daniel del Valle

Process support at CherylStyle: Suzanne Chilson

Text by Nicole Sforza, with editorial support from DD Kullman, Robin Jayn Milne, and Ljiljana Ciric-Hoffmann

Illustrations on pages 10–11, 18, 34, 52, 70, 86, 102, 120, 138, 154, and 172 by Jon Arvizu

Food styling by Rebecca Farr

Prop styling by Robin Turk

All photographs by Lisa Romerein, except the following:
pp. 20–21: Inspiration board photographed by Patrik Rytikangas; photographs from left to right: istockphoto.com/Drbou, istockphoto.com/manley099, istockphoto.com/pixsooz; pp. 36–37: Inspiration board photographed by Patrik Rytikangas; photographs from left to right: istockphoto.com/VeraShine, istockphoto.com/JoeBiafore, istockphoto.com/InkkStudios; pp. 54–55: Inspiration board photographed by Patrik Rytikangas; photographs from left to right: istockphoto.com/SKashkin, istockphoto.com/svetikd, istockphoto.com/kedsanee; p. 64: shutterstock.com/ Margoe Edwards; pp. 72–73: Inspiration board photographed by Patrik Rytikangas; photographs from left to right: istockphoto.com/kcline, istockphoto.com/PetrMalyshev, istockphoto.com/lucop; pp. 88–89: Inspiration board photographed by Patrik Rytikangas; photographs from left to right: istockphoto.com/Sveta, istockphoto.com/hatman12, istockphoto.com/aleaimage; pp. 104–105: Inspiration board photographed by Patrik Rytikangas; photographs from left to right: istockphoto.com/kamrit, istockphoto.com/burwellphotography, istockphoto.com/carolegomez; pp. 122–123: Inspiration board photographed by Patrik Rytikangas; photographs from left to right: istockphoto.com/AnthonyRosenberg, istockphoto.com/wiktory, istockphoto.com/muchemistry; pp. 140–141: Inspiration board photographed by Patrik Rytikangas; photographs from left to right: istockphoto.com/JoeBiafore, istockphoto.com/EricHood, istockphoto.com/kameleon007; pp. 156–157: Inspiration board photographed by Patrik Rytikangas; photographs from left to right: istockphoto.com/Willard, istockphoto.com/coward_lion, istockphoto.com/wragg; pp. 174–175: Inspiration board photographed by Patrik Rytikangas; photographs from left to right: istockphoto.com/nicolesy, istockphoto.com/cclickclick, istockphoto.com/debreny

CherylStyle wishes to thank the following individuals for their participation in the party photo shoots:
Going-Away Roast: Jesse Ochoa, Edwin Sequeira, Lindsay Loisel, Joe Doucett, Bill Smith, and Maria Smith; Zen: Mariel Hemingway, Robert Williams, Anthony Rolfes, Linda Johannesen, Langley Crisman, Ben Smith, and Cameron Crisman; Martini: Jade Johnson, Edward Johnson, Holly Underwood, Bruce Spigner, Vanessa Burgan, A. Burgan, Michael Bayless, James Robinson, Connie Robinson, Joy Johnson, and Geneva Spigner; Scotch & Cigars: Rich Meek, Ted Herbig, Dallas Bennewitz, and Bill Pennington; Tween Spa: Taylor Guittierrez, Stephanie Barney, Krystal Ganvin, and A'lira Underwood; Meet & Potatoes: Gina Buskirk, Peter Ax, Christopher Buskirk, W. Michael Oberfield, Adam Goodman, Beverly Ax, and Stephanie Goodman; Baby Shower: Heather Baker, Vanessa Ramirez, Heather Solano, Serena Montooth, Holly Mueller, Claudia Sieb, Brandi Spiczak, and Cari Oberfield; Thanksgiving: Alyssa Gofonia, Jody Shumway, Jack McKibben, Peggy McKibben, Piper Grant, Lily Grant, Joey Lehman, Rebecca Lehman, Tim Gunnick, and Carey Lehman; Pirate: Nicholas DiPuccio, Amber Meyer, Maddox Bloomenstein, and Robert Hauser; Holiday: Jennifer Ryan, Diana Sullivan, Trish Stark, Sara Bennewitz, Anna Loh, and Molly Larkin

Model bookings: Dani's Agency and Leighton Agency

Melcher Media wishes to thank David E. Brown, Anne Calder, Alissa Faden, Shannon Fanuko, Diane Hodges, Heather Hughes, Liana Krissoff, Nancy Leonard, Lauren Nathan, Austin O'Malley, Julia Sourikoff, and Shoshana Thaler.